How to turn *your*
million-dollar
idea into a *reality*

*(from the man who sold the **MCG**)*

FROM **Imagination** *to* **Implementation**

PETE **WILLIAMS**

Wrightbooks

BICENTENNIAL
1807
WILEY
2007
BICENTENNIAL

First published in 2007 by Wrightbooks
an imprint of John Wiley & Sons Australia, Ltd
42 McDougall Street, Milton Qld 4064

Offices also in Sydney and Melbourne

Typeset in Berkeley LT 11/13.2 pt

© Pete Williams 2007

The moral rights of the author have been asserted

National Library of Australia Cataloguing-in-Publication data:

Williams, Pete (Peter John), 1982- .

How to turn your million-dollar idea into a reality (from
the man who sold the MCG) : from imagination to
implementation.

Includes index.

ISBN 0 7314 0575 7.

1. Entrepreneurship. 2. Creative ability in business. 3.
Organizational effectiveness. I. Title.

658.421

Cover image © Newspix/Damian Horan

Pages 26 and 252 Reproduced with the permission of David Gibb

Pages 28–29 Reproduced with the permission of Yahoo! Search Marketing Australia

Pages 101–102 Reproduced with the permission of Shannon Curtis <www.profitableclothing
retailer.com>

Page 132 'Magical Carpet Ride' by Chris Tinkler, *Sunday Herald Sun*, 3 August 2003, p. 25, The
Herald & Weekly Times. The Herald & Weekly Times Photographic Collection/Faith Nulley

Page 176 Reproduced with the permission of Google Inc.

Printed in Australia by McPherson's Printing Group

10 9 8 7 6 5 4 3 2 1

Disclaimer

The material in this publication is of the nature of general comment only, and does not represent
professional advice. It is not intended to provide specific guidance for particular circumstances
and it should not be relied on as the basis for any decision to take action or not take action
on any matter which it covers. Readers should obtain professional advice where appropriate,
before making any such decision. To the maximum extent permitted by law, the author and
publisher disclaim all responsibility and liability to any person, arising directly or indirectly
from any person taking or not taking action based upon the information in this publication.

Contents

To Mum and Dad,
thanks for providing such a strong foundation

Along with all my family and friends I would like to thank the following people for their guidance, love, support and education over the years.

Fleur Byrt   **Bruce Hultgren** Jon-Michail   Michael Hanrahan

Paul Breen   Jay Abraham   **Adam and Magentaline**

Troy Bowen   *Rohan Merry*   **Robert Kiyosaki**   Tony Stewart

Adam Bowen   Garry and the Gaggle   Tony Robbins

Seth Godin   Scott Ginsberg   Mark Victor Hansen

Sarah Felton   Jonathan Jackson   Matt Tabone and 'the uni-crew'

Glenn Williams   **Brian Tracy**   Robyn Webb

Nev Bray   **Akshay Shah**   Gary Halbert   **Rick Doherty**

Ross Mitchell   Richard Branson   Belinda Stewart

Guy Kawasaki Dale Beaumont   PHIL HODGSON

Trav Madden   Michael Port   NicolE STRANO

Andrew Pickett   Dr Tony Alessandra   **Richard Koch**

Peter Sorenson   Yaro Starak   Brent Hodgson   **Shannon Curtis**

Robert Allen   TORY FAVRO   John Burley   *Camille Howard*

Dan Kennedy   Taz and Amy   Adam Birrel

Sam Corríea   Billi Lim   *The Bartercard Geelong team*

Danny Drake and the cash flow crew

Chris and Abbey   **Rick Frishman**   THE TEAM AT WiLEY

Darren and the MJCC   Dave at Frame-mem

Trevor Price and the Supercats

Tegan Gray   Sport The Library   Simon and Maz

Jade, Ness and Rach   **Matt Barkley**   Ted Whitten Jnr

Max and The Kardinia Picture Framing Team

The Porter Family JAY CONRAD LEVINSON **Christina Posnachiwsky**

Steve McKnight Cindy Cashman   Paul Hartunian

What people say about *How to turn your million-dollar idea into a reality*

I wish I had read this book years ago! Pete's ideas will transform the stuff in your head to the stuff in your wallet. His tips, systems and ideas, combined with his intelligent writing style makes this a must read!

Scott 'The Nametag Guy' Ginsberg (author of How to be That Guy and Make a Name for Yourself <www.hellomynameisscott.com>)

Australia needs more entrepreneurs like Pete Williams to keep the cogs of industry turning and the left-field business fires burning bright. Pete proves that entrepreneurial spirit is alive and well in Australia.

Jonathan Jackson (editor—Wealth Creator magazine)

This book is the bible for those looking to launch a new idea or business. It will save you thousands in lost time and money.

Shannon Curtis (author of The Referrals Marketing Toolkit <www.profitableclothingretailer.com>)

Peter has done a brilliant job with this book, it certainly is a dynamite read. Through various practical examples it proves to all of us that success, both personally and financially, can come rapidly with minimal time and effort. Absorb these principles and put them into practice—they really work!

Dale Beaumont (creator of the Secrets Exposed series, young entrepreneur, best-selling author and international speaker <www.dalebeaumont.com>)

Read this book before you start any entrepreneurial venture. Not only is it full of advice from Pete's remarkable experiences but the lessons are reinforced by real-world examples from various companies, both big and small.

Michael Port (author of Book Yourself Solid: The Fastest, Easiest, and Most Reliable System for Getting More Clients Than You Can Handle Even if You Hate Marketing and Selling <michaelport.com>)

The lessons and techniques Pete has shared in this book will help you gain the competitive edge in whatever business you choose to pursue. It's full of unique street smart marketing ideas that anyone can easily put into place. After reading just one chapter, I felt I received more valuable ideas than I received after reading all the chapters in other books.

Dr Tony Alessandra (author of The Platinum Rule and Charisma <www.alessandra.com>)

You shouldn't be allowed to start a business without reading this book three times. The techniques and secrets Pete shares are worth far more then the cost of the book. You should have read this book yesterday.

Rick Frishman (president of Planned Television Arts and co-author of the AUTHOR 101 series, <www.author101.com>)

Pete is a role model for young entrepreneurs; I suggest every entrepreneur take the time to read his book!

Cindy Cashman (million-selling author, <www.firstspacewedding.com>)

How to turn your million-dollar idea into a reality combines two of my favourite elements in a book—a great story and practical business lessons. When you walk away from reading a book feeling both entertained and educated you know you have found something unique and worth sharing with others. Take my advice, read Pete's unique entrepreneur story and use it as inspiration and motivation to create your own.

Yaro Starak (entrepreneur, <www.entrepreneurs-journey.com>)

Ideas can be found anywhere but turning them into reality is what makes the great difference and that's what Pete's book can help you do.

Billi Lim (author of the no.1 bestseller Dare to Fail <www.daretofail.com>)

From getting your great idea off the ground to making your brand stand out from the crowd, Williams's candid approach in *How to turn your million-dollar idea into a reality* is full of simple and practical advice for budding entrepreneurs.

Camille Howard (editor—Dynamic Business magazine)

Pete Williams is the perfect example of entrepreneurial spirit that should be nourished in our youth—*How to turn your million-dollar idea into a reality* covers many practical gems that will inspire readers to action their dreams and create their realities.

Jon-Michail (Australasia's no. 1 Image Coach and CEO—Image Group International <www.imagegroup.com.au>)

Pete writes with entrepreneurial verve and his simple advice could just inspire you to make a fortune. Great stuff!

Richard Koch (author of the best-selling The 80/20 Principle <www.the8020principle.com>)

Introduction

Eliminate the time between the idea and the act and
your dreams become your realities.

Dr Edward Kramer

My first lesson to all you budding entrepreneurs out there is this:
your business won't start itself. Your fantastic product idea will not
simply materialise in front of you if you wish for it hard enough.
Your great business plan will not magically appear on your desktop
one day, in a file titled 'Guaranteed road to riches.doc'. The first
step to success is *implementation*. This book is about turning your
great idea into a great business.

Million-dollar ideas are everywhere. I know people who have
five of them before breakfast. And we've all had the experience of
having a good idea but not doing anything about it, only to see it
appear six months later courtesy of somebody who got off their
bum. There's nothing worse than the 'that could have been me'
feeling. Million-dollar ideas are not worth a million dollars if they
are still inside your head. They won't make any money there. I'm
going to show you how to turn your million-dollar idea into a
reality—and hopefully a million dollars!

Me at my desk, aged four. I have my phone, my helmet and my teddy — all ready for action!

About me ...

I have always been entrepreneurial. One of my earliest memories is of Mum in the kitchen. I came out and dragged her into the hall to show her what I had drawn on the walls. No, I hadn't drawn a house with a chimney in bright yellow crayon. I had drawn arrows leading to my 'office', so that Mum could find me (or in case any important clients came by). I was about four years old.

Where I really cut my teeth as an entrepreneur was at our holiday place in Ocean Grove; I spent all my summer and Easter holidays there. When basketball card collecting was big, I arranged a huge swap meet at the caravan park—I put advertisements all over the park, arranged stalls, and allowed others to set up stalls at my swap meet. I also set up a TV and video in the window of our caravan, facing outside so kids who had to wait their turn to purchase the rare and collectable cards I had on offer didn't get bored and wander off. It was very successful and I had my first taste of creating my own income. During the whole basketball trading-card fad, I also started a newsletter about basketball trading cards, with stories about cards and their values. In my first week I doubled my number of subscribers. Not many people can claim that! And if I had signed up another two people, I would have doubled my readership again. Unfortunately my cousins Adam and Simon remained my only recipients, but I did learn early about the importance of having a database and keeping in touch with clients.

During another Easter holiday, my cousins and I raised money for the Good Friday appeal: we made a range of greeting cards for the people in the caravan park to purchase. We set up a stall near the toilet and laundry block — to maximise foot traffic. The funny thing was that my aunty, who had the responsibility of sending the money in, actually forgot that year and the money didn't make it. (She saved it and sent it the next year.) I learnt at the age of about 11 that you must have good people around you and advisers who know what they are doing!

When I was 16 my folks and I went to America for a holiday and basketball tour. When we were in Vegas as part of the tour there was a store that put your face onto the body of a famous athlete or model, or on *King Kong*. While my mates were being Michael Jordan or posed with girls in bikinis, I chose to put my face on the cover of a business magazine that had the lead story 'Entrepreneur of the year'—yes, perhaps I'm a bit of a nerd.

I was in high school when I became serious and registered my first business name — Impact Plus. I created websites for my high school, primary school, the Geelong Supercats (yes, you've probably noticed I'm a basketball fan), and a few other businesses.

As you can see, I've had an entrepreneurial streak since before I could spell entrepreneur (though I still get it wrong sometimes). And yes, I am only 24 years old, but that's one of my key points—don't let age stop you! You are never too young, or too old. The experiences I had selling the 'G are the basis for many of the discussions in this book, and I was only 21 when I did it.

When I started down the road to selling the 'G, I had just returned from overseas and had little money or time. I was only in my early 20s, so I didn't have a lot of cash, and I worked full-time. I asked myself, how do I start a business like this? *Impossible*, I hear you say. Well, it's not—and you can do it too. I started with a headline-grabbing idea and used this to generate free publicity. I created systems that allowed me to operate the business with minimal time and financial commitment, and leveraged my efforts using other people's time and skills. And there are many other methods that I used to reach my seemingly unreachable goal. All of this will be covered here, and there are more resources available at my website: <www.preneurmarketing.com.au>.

What's in this book

In this book you will find the lessons I have learnt about business and marketing—from both a practical and theoretical perspective. My MCG venture proves what you can do with a great idea, and I will pass on the knowledge I gained from this, as well as from working with my clients and associates. This book is full of useful facts, examples, quotes, stories and information that will help you get out there and implement your own great idea—from the basics of how to register a business name and finding a market, to setting prices and maximising profits. I will also look at what is one of the single biggest problems for many people—the fear of getting started.

I also believe it is important to have a theoretical understanding of business and marketing. I have studied both at undergraduate and postgraduate levels, read endlessly about business and marketing, and have learnt a lot from my business mentors. I will use this knowledge to provide you with a theoretical background that will help you get your ideas out into the world. I will look at marketing strategies, business planning and structuring, and using what other businesses have done to help you develop your own ideas.

Throughout this book you will notice references to the *From Imagination to Implementation Workbook*. This workbook will allow you to apply what you have read in this book to your business, and when you are finished it will provide you with a powerful tool to help you get your business off the ground. Normally the workbook is priced at $79.95, but a free downloadable version is available exclusively to readers of this book. Go to <www.preneurmarketing. com.au/workbook.php> to get your copy today.

Entrepreneurs

There is more interest today than there has ever been in entrepreneurship. Successful businesspeople are now prominent figures in society, and some are even celebrities. For instance, Richard Branson and his crazy publicity stunts often appear in the media, and Bill Gates is a household name. But these two started out just like most of us — unknown, and with only a small amount of money. They both had great ideas, but, more importantly, they had the drive and the desire to do something with those ideas. Whatever your aspirations, there are valuable lessons to be learnt from people such as Branson and Gates.

Finally, I believe entrepreneurship should not just be about the money. Of course, making money is a major reason why people want to become entrepreneurs, and if you are successful there will be no shortage of it. But you must also enjoy the challenge that comes with the journey — there will be obstacles along the way, and your attitude and level of enthusiasm will determine whether these stop you cold or you find a way around them. Also, you can be certain that there will be hard work involved, especially in the start-up stages. But these aspects only add to the satisfaction when the job is done; remember, if it was easy, everybody would do it.

Find out now how to take your idea from imagination to implementation.

Best of luck,

Pete Williams
Melbourne
September 2006

Chapter 1

From imagination to...

idea conception

> The value of an idea lies in the using of it.
> **Thomas Edison**

Key points

¤ What you do with your idea is just as important as the idea itself.

¤ You don't need special skills to make your business a success, just an idea and some enthusiasm. Anybody can do it.

¤ Don't let an opportunity pass you by.

¤ Work hard to achieve your goals.

Before you can make a start on becoming an entrepreneur, you must have an idea. You can have an earth-shattering, oh-my-god-wait-till-people-hear-about-this idea, but it doesn't have to be. A modest but well-executed idea will go further than a fantastic idea that is poorly implemented. You can also borrow or adapt an idea from elsewhere, as I did.

   Much of what you will read in this book is based on my idea of 'selling the 'G'', as it has become known. So what better place to start than to tell you how it happened?

Selling the 'G

After returning from a stint in 2002–03 working for The Athlete's Foot in the US, I went back to work at The Athlete's Foot in Werribee. The plan was to work there for a few months, before heading back to the US to start a business career. As it was a store in its infancy, I frequently spent morning shifts there by myself, so to keep occupied I often read. One morning I was reading *The One Minute Millionaire* by Robert Allen and Mark Victor Hansen, which is a fantastic read for budding entrepreneurs, and one of the stories it tells is of a New Jersey man who bought pieces of the Brooklyn Bridge in New York.

Paul Hartunian had seen a story on television about part of the wooden walkway being removed from the Brooklyn Bridge because it was old and rotting. Straightaway he had an idea. One of the workers was being interviewed for the story, and in the background Paul could see the contractor's truck with his phone number on the side. Paul contacted him immediately and made a deal over the phone to buy the wood for $500, and it was delivered later that day by the slightly bemused worker. Hartunian made A5-sized certificates detailing the history of the bridge and attached a small piece of the Brooklyn Bridge's timber to it, and began to sell the certificates for US$14.95. He also wrote a press release, which he sent out to the media, and within days he was bombarded with enquiries and interview requests. This initial effort generated publicity for Paul for the next six months, and that was just the start.

Pete's tip:
go your own way
If you do what everybody else does, you'll never be able to set your business apart. Many businesses focus on advertising simply because they think that it's the only way to attract attention to their business. Be different — use publicity to build your business.

I instantly loved the simplicity yet effectiveness of the idea, and began to think about how I could replicate this in Australia. The image of the MCG's redevelopment, which had just begun, came to mind. I thought I might be able to get my hands on some of the timber and replicate Paul Hartunian's venture. I rang Bruce Hultgren, who is one of my business mentors and a good friend. (He runs a business creating programs that use music to help children learn ball skills: <www.billybounce.com>.)

A serial entrepreneur like myself, he saw the dollar signs, and the phone calls to track down the timber began. Eventually we got in contact with the wrecking company that had pulled down the MCG's Ponsford Stand. We were told that not only did the company have some of the timber, it also had rolls and rolls of the crested carpet from the MCC members' section in the Ponsford stand! As a sports fan and a collector of memorabilia, I thought this would be a great chance to preserve a piece of Australian sporting history and make it available to fans, as well as a great business idea.

I arrived the next morning to see and secure the purchase I had made over the phone the previous day. To my amazement the carpet was sitting in the back of the warehouse getting damp; it blew my mind. They also had the bar, which had the MCC logo on it. I negotiated to purchase that also, but later found out that the Variety Club had shown interest and had secured it with another of the warehouse reps the day before—I was not going to argue with a charity. I believe they later auctioned it off and raised a great deal of money for their wonderful organisation.

> The winner is the chef who takes the same ingredients as everyone else and produces the best results.
> **Edward de Bono**

I arranged for a courier to pick up all the timber and carpet and deliver it to my house, in Bacchus Marsh. The carpet lived in the garage for a few weeks, but I was concerned that it would get wet there so the timber and carpet were relocated to the study and the rumpus room.

In the early stages I received a great deal of support and help from an associate and mentor of Bruce's, Phil Hodgson, who, among other things, helped with the idea development and the wording of the plaques that accompanied the carpet. He was a great asset and highly valued. Having good people around to support you is vital.

Although I was initially searching for the timber to make certificates similar to those made by Hartunian, I decided to use some of the timber that I saved to make the frames for a limited number of MCC carpet pieces; that way, they would have even greater value and appeal. My neighbour at the time was a former cabinet maker and unlike my father, who also had a shed full of tools collecting cobwebs, John actually used his regularly, so I enlisted his help to cut the timber. The warehouse had already cut the timber into tongue-and-groove–style flooring, so it was easy for John to turn some of the timber into the required style for framing. While in the US I had purchased a huge range of unframed memorabilia, including pictures and signed photos, and I was in the process of having it all framed by a local sports memorabilia framer, Frame-mem. So Dave at Frame-mem became our framer for the initial series.

The different editions of the framed carpet initially released, with a football and cricket version and different frame options.

With John cutting the timber and Dave making the frames, Bruce and I could spend our time focusing on generating sales and not do any of the construction dirty work. Bruce is an ex-NBL basketball player and seems to know everyone, so we also enlisted the help of one of his contacts who runs Sport the Library (a sports photo library) to find the photos I used in the frames. I paid a royalty for this. I also enlisted couriers to do a lot of the deliveries, again to leverage my time. However, as Bruce worked for himself he did take on the responsibility of delivering a good number of the frames initially. I was still working at The Athlete's Foot, dealing with shoes and feet, so I wasn't as free during business hours, but the way I consciously structured the business allowed for most of the work to be done over the phone or after hours, such as the packing of the frames, which was done in the rumpus room at Mum's place.

I also decided to donate 10 per cent of every frame sale to a charity. We chose the E.J. Whitten Foundation <www.ejwhittenfoundation.com.au>, which supports prostate cancer research, as I felt it had the best fit with what I was doing. Ted Whitten—a former AFL player—was known as 'Mr Football'; he died from prostate cancer in 1995. I initially approached the E.J. Whitten Foundation because I wanted to put some of the profits towards a good cause, but later I also formed a joint venture with the foundation, which is explained in chapter 16.

Pete's tip: share the wealth

Donate a percentage of your profits to your favourite charity. You can help those in need and potentially build your business at the same time.

I created a number of different versions of the frames, to enhance their appeal. The initial release consisted of two styles—one based around cricket and one around footy. The layout of the frames was the same; I simply changed the photos and the wording on the plaque to differentiate between the two. This way I felt I could capture both markets of MCG fans. Each of these styles had two different series—a limited edition of 50 that was framed with authentic MCG timber, and a second series of 500 that had a generic mahogany frame.

I made two or three of each series initially, so that I had stock to ship, but did not restrict our cash flow too much or require a large capital investment (more on this in chapter 7). The framer was able to produce the frames within a great turnaround time. This enabled me to sell the frames with a 14-day delivery—enough time to produce extra frames and deliver them on time—thus working on a make-to-order basis, which is very good for cash flow. I worked out a maximum number of frames for each series, so that they would be limited editions. I also gave away a small piece of green timber, which was taken from the old MCG seating, to add value to the first 50 orders.

I then began to think of the best target market to sell to. Obviously I came to the conclusion that MCC/MCG members would be the perfect market, so I arranged a meeting with the MCG. Unfortunately they didn't like the proposal, and decided not to be involved. However, about three days later the MCG issued a press release announcing that they were going to conduct their own auction of MCC memorabilia and carpet when they began the redevelopment of the MCC Member's Pavilion at the MCG. I guess I'll never know if they leveraged my idea. But by using creative marketing ideas, I generated sales off the back of the publicity the MCC created for themselves.

To start making sales I wrote a series of press releases, one with the heading '21 year old sells MCG for under $500'. I sent these out to every media outlet I could find, and the media onslaught began—Channel 7, the *Herald Sun*, and 3AK, just to name a few. I received a great deal of free publicity with a huge number of articles plugging my idea and venture, which prompted the initial run of sales. (More on this in chapter 10.)

At the same time as my selling the 'G venture was going on I was also involved in a real estate investing 'challenge', which was being run by Steve McKnight <www.propertyinvesting.com>. His first book *From 0 to 130 Properties in 3.5 Years* became a national bestseller, and for his follow-up book he was mentoring a group of budding real estate investors towards the goal of acquiring $1 million worth of property in one year. I was receiving a reasonable amount of press for this too, which involved a number of positive segments on *Today Tonight*.

All this publicity meant I was starting to be recognised occasionally as the guy who was selling the 'G. The feedback was fantastic—everybody thought it was a great idea. One night while I was out in the city catching up with a group of friends from university, and while out at a club a guy recognised me from my various TV appearances. We ended up chatting for a while about what I was up to. I actually walked away at the time a bit disappointed it wasn't, say, Eddie McGuire who had seen me on TV — oh well, any publicity is good publicity as they say ...

At the end of 2004 I moved to Ocean Grove and started using a local framer in Geelong, Kardinia Picture Framers. At the time of writing, some of the timber I bought is being kept in a family friend's garage in Bacchus Marsh. I still have some timber and carpet that is yet to be sold, the venture is ongoing, and you can see what is happening now at <www.sportinglimitededitions. com>. You may be lucky enough to grab a frame or a pen if there are any left. I recently had executive-style hand-crafted pens created from some of the MCG wood, and through my networks have sold a quantity of these to Crown Casino, among others. (More on the power of networks in chapter 15.) I am always looking for new ways to capitalise on the idea and the momentum I have built up.

Download:

Visit <www.preneurmarketing. com.au/mcgaudio.php> to download a short audio file that gives an overview of the selling the 'G venture.

But can I do it?

If you are worried that maybe you are not cut out for this, think again. Anybody can do it. I was not born with these skills, and they certainly don't run in my family. It takes a little ingenuity and creative thinking, but there is no mystery to it. I didn't have any top-secret information or an unusual technique.

To prove that my folks are not businesspeople and that I didn't inherit this ability, when the basketball card craze was in its early stages in Australia we were in a store in the city, and the owner of the store offered a box of cool new cards to my mum and dad on consignment (sale or return) to resell to my mates. Being the *non*-entrepreneurs that they are (nontrepreneurs?), they couldn't see the value and the potential of this offer and they knocked it back. Basketball cards later became hugely popular. I still remind them about that, and the money they lost.

So what are you waiting for?

There it is—an overview of how I sold the 'G. It's not rocket science, just a great idea, some hard work and creative thinking. To summarise:

¤ I took an idea from overseas and adapted it to the Australian market.

¤ I used free publicity to generate sales.

¤ I worked on a make-to-order basis to boost cash flow.

¤ I created special and limited editions to generate interest.

¤ I used my contacts to create opportunities.

¤ I leveraged my time by paying others to do some of the work.

These are just some of the strategies that will be examined throughout the book to help you turn your idea into a success story. And anybody can do it, so read on...

Chapter 2

From imagination to ...

fearlessness

Key points

¤ Overcome your fears by redefining failure.

¤ Setbacks are merely a step along the path to success.

¤ Learn from your mistakes.

¤ Overcome a fear of success by getting started.

If you are going to be successful with your business ventures, there is one emotion that you must overcome: fear. Everybody experiences fear at some stage when pursuing their goals. It is the inevitable result of leaving the safe path to go in your own direction. Fears can include:

¤ What if my idea isn't good enough?

¤ What if I'm not good enough?

- ¤ What if something goes wrong?

- ¤ What if people don't like what I'm doing?

- ¤ What if I'm too old? Or too young?

- ¤ What if I go broke?

Feeling like this is natural, and even healthy. If you don't have some concern about what you are doing and an awareness of the possible risks involved, you may be racing into something without the proper preparation — and undoubtedly you *will* go broke. However, all of these fears are part of what is really a single, overriding fear: *what if I fail?* Fear can prevent you from making a start, or it can stop you along the way. How do you overcome the fear of failure so that you can achieve your goal?

You must prepare yourself now, and decide that you won't let setbacks or moments of doubt stop you from reaching your target. No matter how great your idea, how hard you work, or how well prepared you are, there will still be moments when you say to yourself, 'Gee, it would be a lot easier if I just got a job'. When it seems like there's a million things to do and most of them needed to be done yesterday, and everything is going wrong, and it is all up to you, it's only natural to wonder whether you've made the right decision, or whether you've failed. Overcoming these moments and conquering your fears are part of the satisfaction that comes with success.

Pete's tip: what's the worst that can happen?

Do you currently work in a stable, nine-to-five job? Well, the way I see it is that if you have a go but don't make it, the worst that can happen is you'll end up back with a nine-to-five job. As long as you don't make any outrageously stupid decisions, you will have spent some time and money and ended up back where you started. But at least you tried!

Fear of failure

Fear of failure can put an end to the best ideas. In today's world, being a 'success' is very highly regarded. People who have high-paying jobs, big houses and nice cars are generally considered successful. People who tried to start their own business but it didn't work out are usually considered failures. But you can appear to have all the modern trappings of success and still not be successful, and you can appear by conventional standards to have failed without having really done so. What do you think?

I consider people who have the courage to leave the security and comfort of a nine-to-five job and attempt to make it on their own a success. It doesn't matter whether their idea panned out or not — just trying makes them a success. Trying to make your own way takes guts, imagination, determination, willpower and effort. How can such a person be considered a failure?

Would you rather have the high-paying job and nice car, but spend all your time thinking about your business idea? 'If only I could leave this high-paying job and start riding a skateboard, I could open up that cafe that cuts your hair while serving you coffee, washing your car, doing your laundry and reading your stars.' Well, if that's your business idea — good luck! If your dream is to be an entrepreneur and you are not doing it, the job and the car do not make you a success (even though people might see you as one).

There's no such thing as failure

To overcome a fear of failure, you must realise that there *really is no such thing as failure*. Success and failure are merely perceptions. Something that might look like a failure at the moment is only another step towards your eventual success, or even the success itself.

Take the story of the now famous and hugely successful Post-it note. The adhesive used on Post-it notes was invented in 1968 by 3M research scientist, Dr Spence Silver. He was attempting to design a strong adhesive, but he actually 'failed' and the adhesive he developed was very weak. Dr Silver tried unsuccessfully for five years to find a use for his new adhesive. Arthur Fry, a new-product development researcher, attended one of Silver's seminars, and he was intrigued by the strange adhesive. During his spare time Fry sang in a church choir, and it annoyed him that the bookmark in his hymn book would always fall out when he stood up to sing. One day he realised that he had found the perfect use for Dr Silver's glue — it could be used to make a bookmark!

The original Post-it notes were used as bookmarks, and the remaining notes were shown to the 3M marketing department, but they rejected them as useless (a failure). Fry gave them to his secretary to dispose of, but she instead found what is now the typical use for them. Fry told her to distribute the remaining notes to all the executive secretaries in the 3M offices. When they ran out, she was inundated with calls for more. These calls were passed on to the marketing department, who finally got the idea. Initial prototypes were available in 1977 and by 1981, after a large sampling campaign, the product had been introduced around the world.

Everyone now knows of and uses Post-it notes. This is a classic tale of a failure turned into a success. Post-it notes have been developed in a range of colours and designs for a variety of uses, and they can be found in offices, schools and homes all around the world.

Nev Bray, from one of Melbourne's leading building companies, Bray Constructions, tells a story of failing to win a job with a client, but due to the way he conducted himself, he can now attribute over $1.5 million worth of work directly to the client and their referrals. So he didn't get the job he was after, but he did get other work as a result of quoting for this client.

I have not failed. I've just found 10 000 ways that won't work.
Thomas Edison

As an entrepreneur, you are bound to venture into areas that are new to you. How can you not make some mistakes along the way, no matter how well prepared you are and how hard you work? It could even be suggested that if you don't make the occasional mistake, you are not being adventurous enough in your business strategy. Taking calculated risks can be part of creating a successful business.

The nature of all human advancement, both great and small, is that we learn as much from our mistakes as we do from our successes — probably even more. We wouldn't be where we are today if some great minds before us had given up when they ran into problems. Thomas Edison, for example, conducted thousands of unsuccessful experiments before eventually finding a practical design for the light globe. The nature of scientific experiment is that scientists learn from their mistakes, and conduct the next experiment a little differently. This can be done hundreds — or even thousands — of times over, until the experiment is a success. Does this mean the earlier experiments were failures? No, it's just part of the process. No scientist expects to reach a final outcome after only one experiment.

> **Pete's tip: don't make the same mistake twice**
>
> *Mistakes are inevitable. Don't let them get you down, but make sure you learn from them. Then move on.*

Being an entrepreneur or a businessperson is no different — when you run into difficulties, fix them, learn from them and move on. Even a complete business collapse can teach valuable lessons for future success. Many successful businesspeople have previously started or run businesses that didn't do well.

> Failure is only the opportunity to begin again more intelligently.
> **Henry Ford**

Some people who don't know how to fail...

Let's have a look at a few people who refused to accept that they had failed.

As a basketball fan, I'm going to start with Michael Jordan. Jordan is today generally considered the best basketball player ever to step onto a court. He won six championships with the

Chicago Bulls, five league most valuable player awards, numerous scoring titles — you name it, he won it. So what's he doing here? In high school Michael Jordan was cut from the school basketball team. Was he a failure when this happened? Of course not. He just hadn't reached his goal yet. He later said: 'Whenever I was working out and got tired and figured I ought to stop, I'd close my eyes and see that list in the locker room without my name on it'.

Never give up. Never give up. Never give up.
Winston Churchill

Australian author Matthew Reilly had his first novel *Contest* rejected by every major publisher in the country. Undefeated, he decided to publish the book himself. He paid for 1000 copies to be produced, and sold them to bookshops one store at a time. An editor from one of Australia's major publishers bought one of these copies, and she loved it. She tracked Matthew down and signed him up. Matthew has gone on to be an internationally successful author, with his books on bestseller lists all around the world.

Have you read the novel *Catch-22* by Joseph Heller? It is a literary classic, and spawned the now-common phrase 'catch 22'. Why was it called *Catch-22*? Because it was rejected by 21 publishers. It has now sold millions of copies and was turned into a movie. Imagine if Heller had stopped after receiving the twenty-first rejection letter...

Chicken Soup for the Soul is a book of 'powerful tales of ordinary people doing extraordinary things'. It was rejected by 140 publishers! Even the book's agent gave up on it. But authors Jack Canfield and Mark Victor Hansen believed in their book, and kept going. They eventually found a publisher, and went on to sell millions of books. Canfield and Hansen are now among the best-selling business authors of all time.

When Sylvester Stallone finished writing the screenplay for *Rocky*, he tried to sell it with himself playing the lead role. He was unknown at the time, and some studios were interested in the film but would not allow Stallone to act in it. But Stallone held out, and eventually went on to play the boxer in the role that launched his career.

One of the greatest presidents in American history had plenty of chances to be considered a failure, but he wouldn't accept this. Let's see what happened to him:

- born into poverty in 1809

- failed in business in 1831

- ran for the state legislature and lost in 1832

- failed in business again in 1833, and lost money that he had borrowed from friends

- had a nervous breakdown in 1836

- was defeated when running for speaker in 1838

- was defeated when running for elector in 1840

- was defeated when running for Congress in 1843 and 1848

- was defeated when running for the Senate in 1854 and 1858

- was defeated when running for vice president in 1856.

Who was this? Abraham Lincoln. Maybe the fact that he had endured such a hard road to get to the presidency made him so good at the job when he finally got there.

These are just a few examples of rejections or setbacks—which could have been perceived as 'failures' at the time—leading to outstanding success. There are thousands of these stories, and more are being written every day. Maybe you know somebody like this.

> Never confuse a single defeat with a final defeat.
> **F Scott Fitzgerald**

As you can see, overcoming obstacles is a vital ingredient for many successful people from all walks of life. They overcome fears and doubts. They refuse to accept defeat. They instead learn from these events and use them as motivation to keep going until they reach their goals. This is an attitude you must adopt to be a successful entrepreneur. Overcome your fear. See failure for what it is—merely a temporary setback that can lead to greater things. And even if in the end your idea doesn't work, it doesn't mean you have failed. Just trying—where many others do not—makes you a success. Along the way you will have learned valuable lessons that can help you in life or with other ventures in the future.

Learning from your mistakes

Mistakes are an inevitable and valuable part of the process of creating your own business, but to learn from them you must analyse them. When you encounter a temporary setback, ask yourself the following questions:

¤   What was the mistake?

¤   Why did this occur?

¤   Could this have been avoided?

¤   If so, how can I avoid this problem next time?

¤   What lessons can I learn from this?

Find out exactly what went wrong, and why. Don't blame other people who may have been involved; make it clear that you are just trying to find out what happened so that the problem can be avoided in the future. Take responsibility for the problem, and for fixing it.

Discuss the problem with business associates, friends or family. Get some other perspectives and opinions, and find out how other people have handled such problems. Don't be shy or embarrassed—use it as a learning experience. Think about your mistake and learn from it, then move on.

Sally Anderson, a legacy coach for Legacy Leadership <www.sallyanderson.co.nz>, says lessons are sent to us in three phases; first is a tap on the shoulder, then a piece of 4 × 2 to the back of the head if you didn't learn the first time, and then if you still haven't learnt the lesson, it's a Mack truck headed right at you. You may not learn from your mistakes the first time, but if you don't eventually learn from them they will appear as a Mack truck.

Think you are too young? Or too old?

The fear of being too young or too old to become an entrepreneur is not unusual, but there really is no age limit. There are successful entrepreneurs of all ages.

I often hear people in their 20s say they will get their idea off the ground when they have 'settled down'. This amazes me. I actually think it is harder to start after 'settling down'; there may be kids, a mortgage, two cars to run and myriad other responsibilities. Why wait until you have taken some, or all, of these on? Most people in their early 20s don't have these responsibilities, and are therefore better placed to take a chance and try something adventurous.

As I proved with the MCG, you don't necessarily need a lot of money to get started; all you need is a good idea. I was only 21 when we started selling the 'G. Richard Branson has been an entrepreneur since he was a teenager. He started a student magazine, then moved on to selling records via mail order. Bill Gates left Harvard University in his early 20s to concentrate on Microsoft. Alex Tew is the English guy behind The Million Dollar Homepage <www.milliondollarhomepage.com>. He sold one million pixels on a single web page for US$1.00 each. He was only 21 at the time.

> **Pete's tip: age doesn't matter**
> *You are never too young. Or too old. Start today.*

Younger people have the advantages of fewer responsibilities, more energy and more free time, and they often have more creative ideas, as people tend to become more conservative as they grow older.

Just as you are never too young, you can never be too old to be an entrepreneur. Colonel Harland Sanders, the famous colonel behind KFC, didn't start franchising his chicken business until he was 65 years old. KFC is now available in more than 80 countries. Until his death at the age of 90, the Colonel travelled 250 000 miles a year visiting KFC restaurants around the world.

Many older people have the advantage of work and business experience, and are more likely to have money behind them. Retired people also have free time to dedicate to their business idea.

Fear of leaving the nine to five

Another common fear is leaving the safety of a secure job, where you have people to help you, to start a business, where you must be more self-reliant. When you work for a company, you usually have marketing people to do the marketing, accountants to crunch the numbers, and a tech person to help you when you accidentally change the language on your computer to Swahili.

Typically, your profession provides you with skills within one particular field, and this translates to the core idea for starting your business, but you may be worried about your lack of experience in other areas. If you are a plumber and you open your own business, you have the leaky-pipe repairs covered, but what about the marketing, or the tax or the office management? If you are an accountant, you will be able to keep your own books, but you might not know how to manage staff, run an office or develop a marketing plan.

You may be highly skilled in your area, but to run your own business you must also become comfortable with many areas that may be unfamiliar to you. This does not, however, mean that you must become an expert in these aspects of your business. If this is a fear that is holding you back, you must accept that you can't do everything—seek counsel from others who know more than you do, and leverage other people's knowledge and experience (see chapter 7).

You don't necessarily need to hire full-time staff to cover skills that you lack. For example, you don't need an in-house accountant. Just find an accountant who will be at the other end of the phone when you need help, or who will come to see you when you are making a big financial decision. You can hire a bookkeeper who comes in one afternoon a week to take care of the bills and the invoicing. You don't need to be a financial expert yourself, you just need to pick up enough so that you can work with the people who are experts. Once your business starts to expand, then you can think about hiring part-time or full-time staff.

There are businesses or individuals out there who can cover just about any need that arises: marketing, technical support, bookkeeping, legal advice, transport, storage, sales, administration—the list is almost endless. These people and businesses are experts at what they do, so use this knowledge and experience to your own advantage. Don't let the fear caused by your lack of experience across a range of fields hold you back.

Fear of success

Another common fear is the fear of *success*. Sound strange? Well, this is because the fear of success is often mistaken for a fear of failure, but the two are different. Fear of failure is the fear of things going wrong along the way; fear of success is the fear of encountering problems caused by achieving a goal.

Perhaps the biggest of these fears is that people often worry about whether they will be happy once their goal has been achieved. If your aim is to start your own clothing label, thinking about this and planning for it can make you happy, and gives you a goal. Maybe you are dissatisfied in your current job, and enjoy the inspiration of thinking about your business idea. But what happens if you reach this goal, and it isn't as good as you had hoped? What was an exciting idea becomes a disappointing reality. You've left your job, put in the time, money and effort, and you're still not content. This fear is a fear of success. If you're excited and motivated by an idea, it can be safer to hold on to this rather than risk the outcome not meeting your expectations.

> Procrastination is the fear of success. People procrastinate because they are afraid of the success that they know will result if they move ahead now ... it is much easier to procrastinate and live on the 'someday I'll' philosophy.
>
> **Denis Waitley — motivational speaker and author**

How do you overcome this fear? The answer is very simple: get started! You won't know until your business is up and running whether it will make you happy, but it most likely will. I've seen people have this fear before starting, but I've never seen it turn into reality. A very large majority of the entrepreneurs I meet thoroughly enjoy what they do; running their own business is as exciting and challenging as they hoped it would be, and the financial rewards have met or exceeded expectations. Nobody can give you a money-back guarantee that life will be good once your goal is achieved, but I would consider it a very safe bet. You will be working in a field you enjoy, meeting new people, doing new things, and (hopefully) making more money. Who wouldn't enjoy that?

There are, of course, two alternatives. First, don't start your business. Is this likely to lead to happiness? While it might feel safer just to dream about it, sooner or later this will lead to disappointment and regrets. The other option is that you start it and you don't enjoy it. The simple solution is that you stop and return to whatever you were doing before. If this happens, you can at least gain satisfaction from having tried, and you won't spend the rest of your life thinking, 'If only I had given that a go'.

Success also brings responsibility, which people can be afraid of. If you are successful, you will have to run the business, look after the finances, make big decisions, and keep everything moving. You won't have a manager to check things with, and when there are problems it will be your job to sort them out.

Instead of seeing this as something to be afraid of, see it as a challenge. If you have never done these things before, prepare yourself. Read business books. Go to seminars. Find a business mentor. Talk to friends who run their own businesses. Do a short business management course. You must be ready for the responsibility that will fall to you, and accept this as part of the challenge, not something to be afraid of.

The fear of change can also be part of the fear of success. If your business takes off, your lifestyle will most likely change. You might have to work longer hours, especially at the beginning, taking you away from your family or other interests. In the short term, you might have to accept this as part of the price of what you are doing. But, in the long term, if your business does well you should be able to arrange it so that you are not working any longer hours than you did before, and you might even be able to work less. Another bonus is that you might have more flexibility to work when you want, or to work from home. (I believe it is vital to structure your business around your personal goals, discussed further in chapter 4.) Being an entrepreneur rarely involves more interruption to lifestyle than a comparable position working for somebody else.

> The way to get started is to quit talking and begin doing.
> **Walt Disney**

Chapter 3

From imagination to...

finding your million-dollar idea

Ideas are the beginning points of all fortunes.
Napoleon Hill

Key points

¤ Your goal from day one should be to develop a *profitable* business idea. Don't just start a business in your area of expertise without exploring the potential market.

¤ Being an entrepreneur does not necessarily mean creating something completely new.

¤ Adapt an existing product or service and put your own personal spin on it.

¤ Always keep your eyes open for opportunities.

Let's have a look at how you can come up with an idea for your business. This chapter is a 'choose your own adventure' style; if you already have a business idea, only some of the information in this chapter might be useful to you. If you just know that you want to be an entrepreneur, but you have not yet developed an idea, read on! You can start with what I call 'becoming a fisherman'; that is, get out there and see what the world needs. Find a problem that needs solving. Find a hole in an existing market. Or you can leverage somebody else's idea—find an existing product or service and think of a way to do it better.

Here's a little story that I really like, and it reflects how you should read this chapter. Over the years, psychologists have done many, many studies on the effects of positive and negative attitudes—the difference between optimists and pessimists. One such test they did was on a couple of five-year-old boys, named Billy and Johnny.

Billy was a very negative little boy. It didn't matter what was going on for Billy, it was always bad. He was always moaning and groaning about something. Johnny, on the other hand, was always very positive.

Doctors decided to see if the environment would have any effect on their attitudes. So they put the boys into two different rooms and isolated their environments. They took Billy and put him in a room with every conceivable toy a five year old could want. There were trucks and toy guns and water pistols. They left him there to play with the cool toys for an hour.

They took Johnny down the hall and put him in another room, and told him to have fun for about an hour and that they would be back to check up on him. Inside this room was nothing but horse manure; however, they shut the door and left him alone.

About an hour later the psychologists came back to check on the two little guys. When they checked on Billy they couldn't believe their eyes. He was sitting in the middle of the room crying his eyes out, with toys thrown all over the place. They asked Billy what the matter was. Billy said, 'That toy is the wrong colour, that one didn't make the right sounds, that one isn't big enough.' According to Billy, every toy had a fault.

They left him and went down the hall to check on Johnny. When they opened the door to his room they couldn't believe what they saw. Here was Johnny, in a room full of horse manure, laughing and flinging the stuff all over the room and having a ball.

They said to Johnny, 'What are you doing?'

'I'm having a ball like you told me to,' said Johnny.

'But you're in a room full of manure—how can you have fun?'

Johnny replied, 'With all this, there must be a pony in here someplace.'

That's how I want you to read this chapter—have fun and dig around until you find what you need. And if you learn something from Johnny, it will also be a great help to you in your business venture and life—always look on the bright side. No matter what problems you are faced with, look through the manure and find the pony—it's got to be there someplace!

> You've got to look for a gap, where competitors in a market have grown lazy and lost contact with the readers or the viewers.
>
> **Rupert Murdoch**

Profitable ideas

In his book *The Boron Letters*, Gary Halbert writes about one of his lessons on selling. He asks his students, 'If you and I both owned a hamburger stand and we were in a contest to sell the most hamburgers, what advantages would you most like to have on your side?'

The answers are predictable—the best meat, the best location, the lowest prices. Gary tells his students they can have all these advantages, but the only advantage he wants will ensure that he whips the pants off them. What does he want? A starving crowd.

Become a fisherman

If you are looking for a new idea to start a business, ask yourself this simple question: what product or service will give me a starving crowd? Your aim as an entrepreneur should be to develop a product or service that people want. Success and profits will come much more easily if you leverage an existing demand, rather than try to sell something that people aren't interested in.

You must go fishing where the fish are. Develop a product for profitability.

There is no use trying to fish where there are none; find a full pond where they are hungry ...

The best way to develop a venture is to find a market with money that has an unfilled need, then create a product or service that fills that need. One of my favourite examples is incredibly simple—the hammer. You wouldn't give this tool a second thought today, but imagine what a revolution it was when it was invented. Consider how much easier it became to join two pieces of wood together or to hang a picture on a wall. These are the specific uses that a hammer is designed for. Without these a hammer is useless, and it came about because somebody asked, 'What would be an easier way to hang a picture on a wall?' What can you come up with that fills a specific need?

> I never perfected an invention that I did not think about in terms of the service it might give others … I find out what the world needs, then I proceed to invent.
>
> **Thomas Edison**

The internet is a very powerful resource for budding entrepreneurs, both for ideas and as a business tool. You can use the internet to run your business from home or in your spare time, especially when you are starting out. Using the internet also means that you have access to a global marketplace without leaving your computer. And the internet is also a great way to check the demand and size of your potential marketplace. I call this going fishing—you are trying to find out where potential customers are biting.

So how do you do this? It's very simple. Everybody is familiar with using internet search engines—such as Google or Yahoo!—to find something on the net, but you can also use these as a tool to find out what other people—your potential customers—are searching for. Most search engines keep track of the terms people use to search, and how often each term appears.

Pete's tip: develop a *profitable* business idea

If you do what everybody else does, you'll never be able to set your business apart. Many businesses focus on advertising simply because they think that it's the only way to attract attention to their business. Be different— use publicity to build your business.

This information is freely available, and you can use it to gauge the level of interest (often from all over the world) in an idea you have.

A useful site for this is Yahoo! Search Marketing <searchmarketing.yahoo.com>. Simply use the 'Keyword assistant' function, which is free of charge, to find out what people are searching for. For example, for the purpose of writing this book I entered 'sport memorabilia' into the keyword tool and received the results shown in table 3.1.

Table 3.1: searches for sports memorabilia in June 2006

Search term	Count
Sport memorabilia	1126
Collectible memorabilia sport	295
Card memorabilia sport	221
Buy memorabilia sport	54
Sport memorabilia store	32
Sport memorabilia Australia	19
Celebration memorabilia sport	13
Auction memorabilia sport	12
Box car match memorabilia sport	12
Anthony memorabilia Mundine sport	10
Wide World of Sport memorabilia	10
Autographed sport memorabilia	8
Value sport memorabilia	8
Matheson memorabilia New Phil sport Zealand	7
Australia memorabilia payment plan sport	6
Australian sport memorabilia	6
Authentic memorabilia sport	6

Source: Yahoo! Search Marketing Keyword Assistant

Table 3.1 lists how many times these terms have been searched for on this site in a month. If you are thinking of starting up some sort of memorabilia enterprise, you can instantly see that there is a lot of interest in cards.

Are you thinking about starting a photography business? Let's see what happens:

Table 3.2: searches for photographers in June 2006

Search	Count
Photographer	1782
Wedding photographer	1172
Become a photographer	304
Famous photographer	302
Brisbane photographer	290
Wedding photographer Gold Coast	275
Wedding photographer Sydney	268
Wedding photographer Brisbane	260
Melbourne wedding photographer	243

Source: Yahoo! Search Marketing Keyword Assistant

Interesting! You can see that weddings might be the way to go. Here are a few other results from random topics I tried:

¤ When I entered 'dog wash', three of the top seven entries included the word 'mobile'. People obviously expect to have their puppy groomer come to them.

¤ When I tried the word 'mattress' (I have no idea why), three of the top seven entries were about care or cleaning. Maybe you can invent a great new way to clean a mattress?

¤ Are you a handyperson? When I entered 'renovation', 'bathroom renovation' was second on the list, and 'kitchen renovation' was fifth.

¤ Thinking of selling fishing products and you need an area to specialise in? 'Fly fishing' appeared in five of the top ten searches that included 'fishing'.

¤ When I tried 'smoking', the second entry was 'quit' (with a score of 3035), and 'stop' was third (with 1019). There's obviously a lot of people out there wanting to kick the habit. Do you have an idea that will help them?

You can see how this simple keyword search can give you useful information and point you in the direction of what your potential customers are looking for. I consider these keyword tools 'fish finders'. It's not a substitute for detailed market research, but it will help to point you in the right direction when you are trying to come up with, or refine, an idea.

eBay also has a great feature that can help with this, called eBay Pulse <pulse.ebay.com.au>. This will provide you with up-to-the-minute details of what people are searching for, how much people are bidding, what items are most 'watched', and what categories are most popular. Use this as an added fish-finder tool.

Workbook:

Try this keyword search with five different business areas that interest you. Write down the results in your From Imagination to Implementation Workbook, and comment on the results.

You can use this information to come up with a new idea, invention or way of doing things. Find out what people want, and tailor your business around this. It's not always a good idea to simply copy businesses that are already out there. If you do just copy the common ways of doing things, how will you make yourself stand out?

Another useful tool that some search sites have is a facility that allows you to see what current advertisers are willing to pay for a particular search term. Advertisers have to submit bids for keywords, with a higher bid ensuring a more prominent position on a site. If advertisers are willing to pay a high price for a keyword, it's usually a good sign that this particular word is often used in a search, and is therefore potentially a good market. It is usually free to access this service, just to check the bids. (For more information on this, have a look at chapter 13.)

You might also check out some internet chatrooms to see what people are talking about (no, I don't mean 'hotdate.net.au'). There are all sorts of chatrooms available on the net. If you are thinking of starting an accounting business, you are sure to find a chatroom or newsgroup where people talk about tax issues. Log in and see what's going on. What are people talking about? What are people complaining about? What common problems do they have? Do they all think the price of having a tax return completed by a professional is unreasonable? Does poor service seem to be a common complaint? Or errors? Keep in mind that if you see a problem appear, say, 100 times in a newsgroup, you can be sure that there are many more people out there with the same problem.

The internet is a cheap (often free), easily accessible goldmine of information. When you are developing your idea, make sure you are going fishing where the fish are biting. Stack the odds in your favour. This will make it much easier to get your business off the ground, and will make you much more profitable. Don't make it an uphill battle. You must know there is (or will be) a market that is big enough to keep you afloat. If you are starting a retail business, it must be in a location that has buyers. If you create a virtual office that will operate from home or on the net you could have a world market, but make sure there is a market need that you are filling.

> The #1 mistake most businesses make is not having a
> market size that meets their earnings needs.
> **Mark Victor Hansen**

Success with new ideas

Let's see how some people have become successful through their new idea.

Henry Ford was the first person to build factories that used assembly lines, with conveyor belts to move materials. Because of the highly efficient production techniques, in 1916 Ford made over 700 000 Model Ts, which was twice the output of all its competitors combined. This allowed Ford to sell cars much more cheaply than its competitors, and the price of a new Model T actually decreased over the years. Today, Ford is a leading international car maker, and the techniques created by Henry Ford are still being used.

Bette Nesmith Graham invented liquid paper (originally called Mistake Out) in 1951. She was a secretary who had an interest in art, and she thought that if artists could paint over their mistakes, why couldn't typists? She found some paint that was the same colour as the stationery she used, and mixed it with some water. She put this in a bottle, and used a watercolour brush to paint over her mistakes. Soon the invention spread around the office, and—realising the potential—Graham started a part-time business from home selling Mistake Out. She later changed the name to 'liquid paper', and began working in the business full-time. Today liquid paper can be bought all over the world.

There are thousands—maybe even millions—of stories like these. Will people be talking about *your* great invention one day? Use the fish-finding techniques to find out what people want or need, and come up with an idea or invention that will fill that gap. Just creating something new will not guarantee success, you must create something new *that people need and will pay for*.

Building on other people's ideas

Starting a business does not necessarily mean creating a new technology, coming up with something radical that has never been done before or inventing a new product or service from scratch. This is a common misconception. Many would-be entrepreneurs spend years trying to come up with an earth-shattering idea when there are opportunities all around them, every day. Many of the most successful businesspeople all over the world have simply adapted an existing idea, implemented an existing product or service in their own way, or improved on somebody else's creation.

Here are a few of the most successful businesspeople and entrepreneurs of our time, from Australia and around the world: Bill Gates, Richard Branson, Janine Allis, Ben Cohen and Jerry Greenfield, Donald Trump, Anita Roddick, Sam Walton, Rupert Murdoch, John Ilhan and Ray Kroc. All of these people started multi-million-dollar businesses and have become icons in their industries. How many of them invented a new idea, or created a new product? None—not a single one of them. I'll have a look at some of these people later in this chapter, though I'm sure you recognise at least some of the names. And there are thousands more people who have built their success based on other people's ideas.

> Good ideas are common — what's uncommon are people who'll work hard enough to bring them about.
> **Ashleigh Brilliant — English author**

As you've already seen, my idea for selling the 'G was based on Paul Hartunian's idea of selling the Brooklyn Bridge. It wasn't my concept to begin with, but as soon as I read about it I thought, 'How can I do that in Australia?' It just took a bit of searching to find the right opportunity. I made the idea my own by applying it to the MCG and doing it my own way.

Let's have a look at some people who have been very successful using this approach, and then see how you can put it to use.

Pete's tip: ideas are commodities

Ideas are commodities; it's the execution and implementation that makes the true difference in life and business.

Success without reinventing the wheel

Perhaps one of the greatest examples of leveraging an existing idea is that of Bill Gates and Microsoft. Gates has become one of the richest people in the world (his personal fortune is measured in the billions) based on *somebody else's idea*. That's right, the product that started it all for Bill—called DOS, which stands for disk operating system—was not Bill's invention.

In 1980, IBM was building the first commercially viable personal computer, and it needed an operating system to run it. IBM approached Microsoft, which agreed to supply the software — the design for which it bought from Seattle Computer Products for around $50 000. There were several different computer companies and operating systems in the early days, but Microsoft and IBM went on to dominate the industry worldwide, thanks in a large part to DOS, which was the best operating system at the time. Years later, Bill Gates borrowed another idea from Apple computers. Microsoft launched a new operating system called Windows, which used an icon-based system and a mouse instead of text commands to run a computer. Apple had been doing this for years, but it was a revolution for Microsoft users.

Coca-Cola started in the same way. Coke was invented by Dr John Pemberton in Atlanta in 1886. He made efforts to promote the drink, but it did not take off. During the first year, he sold an average of just nine drinks per day. He later sold the rights to the drink to businessman Asa Candler. By 1892, Candler's flair for marketing had boosted sales nearly tenfold. Today, Coca-Cola operates in over 200 countries and has almost 400 brands.

While travelling, Janine Allis recognised that Australia suffered from a lack of wholesome fast-food alternatives. She often had trouble finding something healthy to eat or drink when she was in a hurry. Janine thought the American juice bar trend could be brought to Australia, so she developed a business plan and raised $250 000 through friends who were willing to invest in her idea. She consulted nutritionists and naturopaths to come up with natural, healthy juice recipes. In 2000, the first Boost Juice Bar opened in Adelaide, and since then over 170 stores have opened throughout Australia and New Zealand. Janine found a great idea overseas, and successfully implemented it in Australia.

Richard Branson has never invented anything in his business career. He has run a record label and an airline, opened music stores, released a brand of cola, and now offers financial services, among other ventures. None of these are new ideas. So why has he been so successful? Perhaps more than any other businessperson, Richard demonstrates what can be done with a bit of imagination, a lot of marketing and putting your own personality into your business. His company name — Virgin — attracts attention instantly and he is a shameless promoter, using sometimes outrageous publicity stunts to advertise his brand. He appeared in a wedding dress to open his bridal store, and he drove a tank down Fifth Avenue in New York to introduce Virgin Cola in America. Across all his products, the thing he is selling most is his brand, Virgin.

Richard also likes to move into areas where he believes the existing companies are providing poor service, and give the industry a shake-up. This is one of the reasons he started his airline and mobile phone businesses.

> I want Virgin to be as well known around the world as Coca-Cola.
> **Richard Branson**

Australian John Ilhan has made his fortune selling mobile phones. There's nothing new about mobiles, but there was something new about the way John went about it. The name Crazy John's came about through John's crazy marketing ideas, which included being the first to sell a mobile phone for $1 while his competitors were still charging $200, and holding midnight barbecues for customers. By applying his own personality to selling a common product in an extremely competitive market, John has expanded from a single store in 1991 to over 100 stores today.

Jim Penman started Jim's Mowing in 1982 with a second-hand lawnmower and a trailer. Today, he has over 2300 franchisees in three countries, and Jim's is one of the largest home-service franchises in the world. He didn't create a new business idea, he just improved on an existing one, with his focus on customer service.

In 1948, brothers Richard and Maurice McDonald opened their hamburger restaurant in San Bernardino, California. Its success was based on its limited menu and rapid service. But are the McDonald brothers responsible for McDonald's dominating the fast-food market around the world? No, that honour goes to Ray Kroc, who sold milkshake mixers. Ray heard about the McDonald's hamburger store, and how it ran eight milkshake mixers at a time.

He jumped in his car and went to investigate. When he arrived, the store was doing a roaring trade, and Ray had never seen customers served so quickly. He immediately saw the potential of the store's unique methods, and suggested to the brothers that they open more restaurants. When they asked him who could do that for them, he replied, 'What about me?'

Ray opened the second McDonald's restaurant in Illinois in 1955. There are now more than 30 000 McDonald's restaurants in 119 countries around the world—all thanks to Ray! McDonald's later added another innovation to the fast-food world—the 'drive-thru'. This was an idea that had first been used by banks throughout the US, with drive-thru access to tellers.

Here's another successful adaptation of an existing idea. FedEx is the largest express courier company in the world. It didn't invent postage or courier services, but it changed the way it was done. On its website, FedEx notes the following 'firsts' that it has achieved. It was the first courier company dedicated to overnight delivery, and delivery by 10.30 am the following day. It introduced Saturday deliveries and time-definite services, and was the first to provide money-back guarantees and free proof of performance.

Frederick Smith, the founder of FedEx, didn't invent a new product or service, he just found a better way to provide an existing service. The company began operating in 1973, with the launch of 14 small aircraft from Memphis International Airport. On its first night, Federal Express delivered 186 packages to 25 American cities. FedEx has grown into a worldwide, $29 billion network of companies, offering transportation, e-commerce and business services. (The story around the camp fire is that Frederick Smith wrote an essay based on the FedEx business model while at university—and was given an F!)

Dell Computers is the largest personal computer manufacturer in the world. But Michael Dell certainly did not invent the PC, he just came up with a better way to sell it. Dell started out working in his college dorm room, with just $1000 and the idea of providing affordable computers to college students. His business is now based on direct sales—there's no retailer between the company and its customers, allowing Dell to keep its costs down. Today, Dell has annual revenue of over US$40 billion.

Some of the largest and most successful companies in the world were started either by buying somebody else's idea or simply creating a better way of doing something. There is nothing wrong with this—it is a common approach to business, and as you can see from these examples, it can be an extremely profitable one.

It is my strong belief that ideas are commodities. A car is a commodity, a microwave oven is a commodity, a mobile phone is a commodity and an idea is a commodity. It is there to be developed and used, and it can be bought and sold. If you see an idea that is not being used to its full potential that you think you can do better with, or an idea that may already be successful but you can adapt for your own purposes, then do it! You don't have to reinvent the wheel.

> **Pete's tip: make it you**
>
> *Think about it—everyone has had the same million-dollar idea as someone else. The one who banks that million dollars is the one who implements and executes.*

Don't take it to the extreme of course; you can't simply *copy* somebody else's idea. What I'm talking about is adapting or leveraging an existing good idea and making it your own. You can't open a juice bar and call it Boooost but you can look at how Boost was started and apply it to, say, opening a bakery. You can't open a mobile phone store and call it Crazy Jan's, but you could study what John Ilhan has done and, for example, apply these ideas to an online mobile phone store, or to a different product all together.

Adapting an idea

As we saw with John Ilhan and Richard Branson, injecting your own personality and methods into a business can be a great road to success. If you have strong marketing skills, these can be useful in any business. But you might also have a particular skill that can be applied to a certain product or service. You might, for example, have a secret recipe for spectacular pizzas. Pizza delivery places are everywhere, but maybe your recipe will give you an edge. Or maybe you are a mechanic with an interest in a certain type of classic car. Perhaps you could start a mobile business based on this, specialising in cars that your typical mobile mechanic would not be able to handle.

Adapt and modify things that are already out there. What special skills or talents do you possess? Can you cut hair a better way? Service a car a better way? Paint a house a better way? There are *always* different and better ways to do things, no matter what it is. If existing businesses had every corner of the market covered, there would not be room for people like Richard Branson, Janine Allis, John Ilhan and Michael Dell to make their fortunes. They saw a hole in the market and they moved to fill it, either by adapting a product or selling an existing product or service in a better way.

> A fax machine is nothing but a waffle iron with a phone attached.
> **Grampa Simpson**

Buying an idea

You might find an opportunity if you see somebody else trying to run a business or sell a product or service but not doing a very good job of it. Just look at what happened with Coca-Cola and Microsoft. Does your next-door neighbour have a great idea for an internet-based business, but she doesn't seem to be doing anything about it? Or maybe one of your colleagues has an idea for a mail-order cosmetics business, but doesn't have the skills to put it in place. Perhaps the nursery down the road is really good but its marketing isn't. People have good business ideas every day but don't do anything with them, or implement them poorly. This doesn't make the idea bad, just the execution.

Like anything else, ideas can be bought and sold. Always keep an eye out for potential opportunities. You never know where you might find a great idea. If you come across a product or service that has unfulfilled potential, see if you can get onboard, or take it over. For more on constructing joint ventures, be sure to check out chapter 16.

A long, long time ago...

Okay, so it's not really business related, but I had to include the example of *Star Wars*. George Lucas's groundbreaking movie was inspired by a Japanese film called *The Hidden Fortress*, which is a story about a princess fleeing through enemy territory, escorted by a brave warrior and two squabbling friends. The similarities to *Star Wars* are obvious; a central part of the film is the rescue of the princess from the evil empire, and the hero is accompanied by two bickering robots, C-3PO and R2-D2.

Still no idea?

If you are really stuck for an idea, have a look at network marketing (also known as multi-level marketing). Network marketing is when you are given products to sell for a company and receive payment for this, and you also attract other people to the business. When these people sign up and start selling the products as well, you also receive a payment for the sales they make, on top of your own sales. You can see where the term 'network marketing' comes from.

This type of business gives you the opportunity to leverage off someone else's model and still create your own business or second income, often part-time. Using an existing business idea that has already been tested and has proved successful is a great way to get started and learn sales, business and marketing skills. It's a great stepping stone to your own venture.

The biggest advantage of network marketing is obvious: you will receive an income from the work of others without having to hire them as employees. Other advantages of network marketing are:

¤   You can start in your spare time, and build it to a full-time job if you wish.

¤   It usually doesn't require a large amount of capital to get started.

¤ You can work from home, and control the hours you work.

¤ You have the marketing support of the network marketing company you are working with.

Probably the most well-known network marketing company is Amway. Others are Nutrimetics, Avon and Goji juice, and there are many more out there. If this interests you, type 'network marketing' into a search engine and see what comes up, and then contact the companies for more information.

Another way to leverage an existing business is to buy a franchise. This can involve significant capital outlay, but you will be buying a tested business model and the support of the company you purchase the franchise from, while still owning your own business. There are many different types of businesses that can be bought as franchises, including fast-food outlets, shoe stores, bookstores, lawnmowing services and car washing services.

Workbook:

If you are interested in network marketing or franchising, perform an internet search and find three different companies that interest you. Write down the strengths and weaknesses of each in the appropriate place in your From Imagination to Implementation Workbook, *and then pick the one you think is best for you. Explain your reasoning.*

Most successful entrepreneurs get their ideas for their businesses by studying niche markets and then developing a product or service that meets their needs or solves common problems.

Corey Rudl — author of *The Insider Secrets to Marketing your Business on the Internet*

Chapter 4

From imagination to ...

standing out and making a name

> Starting out with a weak business name is like trying to golf with only one club in your bag. You may sink some shots but it will be a whole lot harder.
>
> *Canadian Small Business Guide*

Key points

- ¤ You must have a unique selling proposition to be successful.

- ¤ Your unique selling proposition should tell your customers what you are offering that your competitors aren't.

- ¤ Your name should communicate what you do.

- ¤ Your name should be memorable, easy to recognise and suited to your target market.

Okay, so you've come up with the million-dollar idea you want to implement and retire on. In this chapter we are going to look at making you stand out from the crowd and choosing your business and/or product name.

Standing out with your unique selling proposition

So you have an idea to market a nuclear-powered mouse trap or, like a few of the entrepreneurs mentioned earlier, you are going to market an existing idea more effectively. You need to be able to clearly communicate what sets you apart from your competition. Whether you call it a unique selling proposition (USP), strategic competitive advantage or differentiating statement — and there are many more — you need to define it.

The concept of having a USP was developed by Rosser Reeves over 60 years ago, in an attempt to distinguish similar products from one another. (Reeves is now in the Marketing Hall of Fame.) What do you stand for and why is your business different? Ask yourself a simple question — why will my clients come to me and not my competitors? If you can answer this, you have your USP. It is a statement of benefit, a consumer's buying motive, a strategic competitive advantage; whatever you want to call it, you must define it. If you can't identify it, how will your customers? Your USP can be included in the title of your business, or as a catchphrase or slogan. I know you have probably heard this before, but that is because it's so important.

Have a think about stores that you go to regularly. Why do you go back to them? Is it the service? The prices? The range of products? You probably go to different stores for different reasons; you might go to the supermarket for the prices, while your favourite hardware store might be a little bit expensive but offers excellent assistance with your backyard projects. Price is most important for one type of store, but it's the service that attracts you to the other. If you are spending $5000 re-landscaping your backyard, getting good advice is more important than saving $200.

Many attempts to communicate are nullified by saying too much.
Robert Greenleaf — management expert and author

Finding *your* USP

Think about what USP means: *unique* selling proposition. This must be something that only you can offer that is useful to your market. Good service is not a USP—the *best* service is. Cheap prices are not a USP—the *cheapest* prices are. A pizza shop that delivers has no USP—a nursery that delivers might. Phone help available 24 hours is not a good USP for a furniture store, but it might be for a vet. Find the USP that suits *your* business and *your* market, and incorporate it into everything your company does—from changing the lining of the rubbish bin, to issuing gift vouchers, to advertising. Make your USP succinct and memorable, so that your clients will remember it and instantly recognise your business.

Pete's tip: find your USP

If you don't know what your USP is, your customers won't know either.

The areas you can base your USP on are:

¤ *Selection*: 'The average widget store carries three to seven widgets, some even have as many as 15 widgets, but our store always has 27 different types of widgets in stock.' For example, Blockbuster's 'Get it first time or get it free' offer. Their USP is that they have more copies of each movie than their competitors.

¤ *Service*: 'Willy's Widgets has 12 expert widget staff to assist you with your every need.' Or, 'We will be at your door within two hours, guaranteed'. For example, FedEx stands for, when it absolutely, positively has to be there overnight. This was a FedEx innovation.

¤ *Price*: 'We always have $50 widgets for sale at $34.' Or, 'We will beat any price by 10 per cent'; for example, Bunnings Warehouse—their USP is that they will always be cheaper.

¤ *Quality*: 'We simply make the best widgets, regardless of cost.' For example, BMW—'Sheer driving pleasure'. Do you think 'We will beat Mercedes's prices by 10 per cent' would work for BMW? Of course not. Part of what BMW sells is prestige, which means it doesn't have to concentrate on price. In fact, expense is expected in this market.

A company that is more profitable than its rivals is exploiting some form of advantage.
Wikipedia

Look at the business from the perspective of your customers — what will be the most important feature of your business for them? If you wish to portray an upmarket image, you can use words such as 'exclusive' or 'quality' to describe your USP. If your service is fast, use 'rapid', 'quick' or 'speedy'.

Here are some questions that you can ask to help find your USP:

¤ Do I have a bigger range of products than my competitors?

¤ Do I have the cheapest prices?

¤ Do I have the best service?

¤ Do I have the quickest service?

¤ Do I offer a service that nobody else does?

¤ Do I have the best quality?

¤ Do I offer a longer warranty or guarantee?

¤ Do I have expert staff?

¤ Do I have discounts for regular customers?

¤ Do I open on weekends or have extended business hours?

¤ Do I have 24-hour telephone support?

These are just to get you started; the list is almost endless.

Your USP should only be a sentence or two long. You want it to be short and catchy so that people remember it and you can use it in your marketing.

Let's have a look at some more USPs:

¤ FedEx: 'When it absolutely, positively has to be there overnight'. (Yes, I know everybody uses this one, but that's because it's so good.)

- ¤ BMW: 'Sheer driving pleasure'.

- ¤ Safeway: 'The fresh food people'.

- ¤ Hungry Jack's: 'The burgers are better'.

- ¤ Blockbuster video: 'Get it first time or get it free'.

- ¤ On Hold Advertising: 'Turning your callers into customers'.

- ¤ Sporting Limited Editions: 'Own your own piece of the 'G'.

If you operate in a very price sensitive market and your products are cheaper than your competitors', use this as your USP. But be aware of your product and your target market. Focusing on price is good for selling toothpaste or milk, but for a person booking a courier to deliver an important package, reliability will be more important than price. And for upmarket products, being seen as cheap can actually be a disadvantage, because high prices can imply quality and exclusivity. Competing on price is okay for Toyota and Holden, but it's not part of the strategy for Porsche or Mercedes. I want to own a Porsche one day and I don't care how much it costs. The expense is actually part of the appeal—owning one means I've reached my goals.

Workbook:

In your From Imagination to Implementation Workbook, write down 10 words that will describe your business. Think about it from the point of view of your customers. Now choose three of these words that you think will appeal most to your customers. Is one of these your USP? Explain your reasoning.

If you're having trouble finding a USP for your business, then you are going to have trouble staying in business. If you haven't been able to find your USP, consider adding something to your business idea that will set it apart from the others so that customers will come back. Remember, other businesses are called competitors for a reason—they are trying to beat you, and they will succeed if you don't differentiate yourself from them.

To open a shop is easy, to keep it open is an art.
Chinese proverb

Here's the most important part of your USP: *you must deliver what you promise.* Your USP will mean nothing if you don't live up to it, and nothing is worse for the reputation of your business than misleading people. This applies to all areas of your business operation, not just your USP.

Hitting the target with your business or product name

Your business or product name is more than just a title—it is a vital marketing tool that can have a significant impact on your business. It positions you in the marketplace and is often the first contact you will have with potential clients and customers, whether it be by an advertisement, by word of mouth or whether they see one of your products. Your name says a lot about your company; a well-chosen name will appeal to your target market, will be easy to remember and will tell people what you do. A poorly chosen business name will be difficult to remember, will be hard to spell, will not reflect what you do and will be unappealing to the people you are trying to reach. Also, your name is very rewarding as it marks the birth/label/title of your idea and business. So what makes a good business name?

Workbook:
If you are having trouble finding your USP, use your From Imagination to Implementation Workbook *to write down five things you could add to your business that would solve this problem. Explain how each one would attract customers, and how it differs from existing offerings of other companies.*

(In this chapter we are just going to look at choosing a good name; the technical side—such as registering a business name and a domain name—is addressed in chapter 9.)

If you do build a great experience, customers tell each other
about that. Word of mouth is very powerful.

Jeff Bezos

Choosing the best name for your business will depend on many
things, including the products or services you offer, your target
market, your USP and what you want the image of your company
to be.

Let's have a look at some guidelines for choosing a good
business name. (These principles can also apply to choosing good
names for your products or services.)

Communicate what you do

The first thing your business name must do is communicate the
kind of products or services you offer. Sound simple? Well, this is
something that some businesses have trouble with. You are at an
immediate disadvantage if people have to make an effort to find
out what you offer, and often they *won't* make the effort, especially
if your competitors are more appropriately named than you.

Have a look at the shops in your local shopping centre next
time you go down the street. I bet there will be a few for which
you can see the name on the front of the store but you still don't
know what they sell. Why would you take the time to find out
when there are plenty of businesses out there that make it easy
for you by reflecting what they do in their name? If you hadn't
heard of either of them before, would you go to Dan Murphy's
or Liquorland to buy a bottle of wine? And again, if you didn't
know the businesses, would you go to Leading Edge Music or
Sanity to buy a CD? Or Burger King or McDonald's if you wanted
a hamburger? (Yes, of course McDonald's has gone on to be rather
successful—please don't send me abusive emails—but do you
think when Ray Kroc was trying to open those first restaurants
years ago, his job would have been just a bit easier if the stores
were called McDonald's Burgers?)

In his book *No B.S. Business Success*, Dan Kennedy gives the
example of customers he knew of who went to Kwik Kopy to
have their photocopying done, but went to another store for

their printing, not realising that Kwik Kopy did both. Kwik Kopy would not have had this problem if it was called Kwik Kopying and Printing. Think about how much business it may have lost simply due to its name.

Communicate how you do it

Your name can also communicate the type or style of product or service that you offer. The Reject Shop leaves little room for doubt. You're not going to go there to buy your partner a Christmas present (I hope), but you might go there to buy a cheap present for the office Kriss Kringle. Minuteman Press and Snap Printing sound like they could do your job quickly. People often need printing turned around rapidly, so these businesses have obviously thought carefully about their names. And the name Lube Mobile certainly sounds as if the company's staff come to you, which is handy because the problem with dropping your car at the mechanic is getting home. Video Ezy sounds like it's going to be, well ... easy, whereas Civic Video sounds a little dull. Pizza Lovers sounds great, but Domino's Pizza? This is where you can think about factoring your USP into the name of your business.

Think about your market

The name is part of your company's image. If you are going to open a vehicle workshop that specialises in large vehicles, you wouldn't call it 'Bob's Friendly Mechanics', but if you were opening in a suburb that had an ageing population or a large number of families, and you wanted these people to be your customers, this could work. People are often wary of going to see a mechanic because most people know very little about cars and are worried they will be taken advantage of. Customers will feel more comfortable going to a friendly mechanic. Truck drivers, on the other hand, will feel more comfortable going to 'Bob's Big Rig Fix-It Shop'. Think about the people who make up your market and what will appeal to them.

Using your own name in the business title can be a good approach if you want to build a close one-on-one relationship with clients, but before you go down this path you have to ask yourself a couple of questions, such as:

1   *Can I personally deal with every client?* By making your name the business's name your clients are going to want to deal with the boss, the chief, the person in charge. Are you going to be able to offer this? Hopefully, your business will grow beyond your one-person band. If you are working towards that, you may find yourself alienating clients who come to deal with you and you only!

2   *Are you planning on selling the business?* You may think this is a premature question given that you haven't even sold one unit yet, but it's still something to think about. If you are hoping to grow the business, it would be best to build a 'brand' around a specific business name, not yours. Bob's Mechanic would probably need to change its name if Bob left, and there goes a lot of brand awareness.

Yes, there are examples where using a name has worked well; take Jim's Mowing and Dick Smith, for example. With anything in life there are exceptions to the rules, but the rules will win 9987 times in every 10 000.

Make it easy to spell and remember

Do you remember the film *The Shawshank Redemption*? Great film, but what was going on with the title? Difficult to spell. Difficult to remember. It's even difficult to say. Gives no idea what the film is about, unlike the movie *Snakes on a Plane*. Company names are no different. You need a name that comes easily to mind—it doesn't get much simpler than Jim's Mowing or Burger King or Text Publishing.

Pete's marketing tip: keep it simple
Don't make your business name cute, clever or trendy, because after people have heard it a few times, it won't be any of these things.

Research conducted by Strategic Name Development in the US found that products with difficult names—such as Touareg, the Volkswagen 4WD—required much more marketing to develop recognition. Maybe Touareg is simple to remember in

Germany (where Volkswagen is based), but it doesn't translate well into English, and the car could easily have been renamed for English-speaking markets.

Choosing letters

I personally am not sure of the strength of the concept of choosing certain letters to signify particular themes in brand names and how it relates to your customers opening their wallets, but another survey conducted by Strategic Name Development examined exactly this. The survey found:

- The letter Q portrays innovation (possibly because it is not a commonly used letter), which works for companies such as Quicken, the software company.

- The letters C, S and B are considered 'classic', which helps companies such as Coca-Cola and Blockbuster.

- L and V are considered 'feminine' (L'Oreal, Victoria's Secret).

- X is considered 'masculine', complex and innovative (Xbox). It is also often considered sexy and exotic. (Have you noticed the number of cars that use the letter X in their title?)

Bill Lozito, co-founder and President of Strategic Name Development, said, 'This recent research on specific letters of the alphabet provides knowledge and insights as to why some names have greater target market acceptance than others'. (Go to <www.namedevelopment.com> for more information on this research and other useful articles.) Have a think about your target market and how you might be able to choose appropriate letters in your company name.

Can your name become a verb?

Can your company name be used as a verb? This is unlikely to play a major role in selecting your name, but it's an interesting idea. For example, the word 'google' has come to mean 'search the internet', so now people often say, 'I'm going to google that to see what I can find'. Other terms that are sometimes used in the same way are Xerox (to photocopy something) and Hoover (to vacuum).

Here is what I hope to see in the dictionary in a few years' time, based on my business Preneur Marketing:

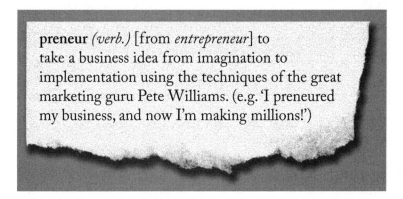

preneur *(verb.)* [from *entrepreneur*] to take a business idea from imagination to implementation using the techniques of the great marketing guru Pete Williams. (e.g. 'I preneured my business, and now I'm making millions!')

Amazingly enough, just after I wrote the above paragraphs, I discovered that the latest *Merriam-Webster Dictionary* includes the word 'google' (lower-case 'g'), which means to use the well-known search engine to look for information on the web. So there you go — Google made it into the dictionary! Will you be there one day?

Some examples

Magazines are fantastic at 'affirmative naming'. Think about these titles:

¤   *Smart Investor*

¤   *Wealth Creator*

¤   *Better Homes and Gardens*

¤   *Entertainment Weekly*

¤   *Australian Gourmet Traveller*

¤   *Australian Wine Selector*.

Is there any doubt about what these magazines contain? Your business name must have the same level of instant recognition.

Another group that is really good at creating names that capture people's interest and create relationships with customers is professional sports teams. They often choose a nickname that connects them to, or reflects, the communities they represent, which solidifies the connection with their fans (customers). For example, Fremantle Dockers (Australian Football League), Miami Heat (National Basketball Association, located in the warmth of Florida), Toronto Maple Leafs (National Hockey League), San Antonio Spurs (National Basketball Association, located in Texas), and Houston Rockets (National Basketball Association, Houston we have a problem).

As a side note and at the risk of drawing a long bow — and an insight into my humour — a funny example of how a well-chosen name can possibly create strong customer loyalty, during the 2004–2005 NBA basketball season in the US in a game between the Detroit Pistons (the city is the centre of American automobile manufacturing, hence Pistons) and the Indiana Pacers, a group of Detroit Piston fans (customers) got into a fight with the Indiana players during the actual game. I am not sure if you choose a 'winner' of a name your customers will go to war for you like the Pistons fans, but maybe if Kmart changed its name to something that related to its customers more, you would see Kmart shoppers beating up the store clerks of Target! Okay, so maybe the fight didn't break out because of the names but you can see what happens when you have loyal fans (customers).

Download:

For a free report on how to use your business name in your advertising, go to <www.preneurmarketing.com.au>

Just for interest, and to possibly contradict some of these lessons, let's see how some companies have come up with their names:

- Adidas comes from the founder's name, Adolf (Adi) Dassler.

- The name Coca-Cola comes from the coca leaves and kola nuts used as flavouring. The K in kola was changed to C to make the name look better.

- Apple computers wanted a name that was distinct from the technical and unfriendly names of most computer and technology companies.

- IBM stands for International Business Machines.

- Nike is the Greek Goddess of Victory.

- The name Microsoft comes from combining microcomputers and software.

- The name IKEA was formed from founder Ingvar Kamprad's initials (IK) plus the first letters of Elmtaryd and Agunnaryd, the farm and village where he grew up.

- Google's name is a play on the word 'googol', which refers to the number one followed by one hundred zeroes.

- Jim's Mowing was so named after Jim conducted years of extensive research into the best way to spell Jim and the best way to describe his business.

There are many ways to create a business name. What's important is that the name you choose portrays who you are, what you do, and how you do it. It's how people identify you; don't make it an obstacle.

> A remarkable name for your organisation, product or service is like pornography: It's hard to define, but you know it when you see it.
>
> **Guy Kawasaki**

The domain game

In the world of the internet, where we now live, you should not create a business without utilising this great business tool. One thing to think about when choosing a winning name is what domain names (internet addresses) are available. It's not the best situation to be in if you choose a winning name, then can't find a 'clicks and portals' (domain) name that is at least close to your 'bricks and mortar' (real world) one. (For more on registering domain names see chapter 9.)

Comparing and testing names

What happens if you have a stroke of genius and come up with two names you love? The obvious answer is to test them. Ask your friends, family and colleagues which name they prefer. Also, the internet offers a way to instantly test two names against each other worldwide with your target audience.

Google Adwords and Yahoo! Search Marketing are services that allow businesses to advertise their sites on search engines, but with a little creativity you can use these services to test anything from headlines to business or product names. Adwords and Search Marketing offer what is termed 'pay-per-click' advertising. This is where you—the advertiser—only pay when someone clicks on your link when it is displayed on a search engine. You don't pay when it appears, only when someone is interested in your advert and clicks on it to visit your site. So what you can do is run two pay-per-click adverts at the same time on these services and see which one generates the most clicks (referred to as a 'click-thru rate'). When people

Workbook:

If you haven't thought about your domain name yet, write down five domain names that would be a good fit for your company in your From Imagination to Implementation Workbook, *then jump on the internet and see if they are available. If they are, think about registering one of them now. You don't have to wait until your business or website is ready, and this will make sure you don't lose the name to somebody else.*

search for words relating to your product, both of your ads will appear, with the different business or product names, and your consumers will instantly tell you which headline, or name, is more compelling by the amount of clicks each name receives.

Here are examples of two of my ventures over the years.

Download:

For a free report on how to conduct split-testing using search engines, visit: <www.preneurmarketing. com.au/splittestonline.php>.

IMPACT PLUS

As mentioned earlier, one of my first businesses was a website design company, which I named 'IMPACT PLUS'. Clients who used my services to create a website and online presence wanted their site to make an impact and impression, but I wanted to convey I could offer more than that, hence the PLUS.

On Hold Advertising

One of my most recent ventures is a company in the telecommunications sector, where the lead product is on-hold marketing message systems. It amazed me when I heard the statistic that 94 per cent of marketing budgets are spent on making the phone ring (including websites, magazine adverts and ads in *Yellow Pages*) with very little spent on securing the sale when a prospect does ring. On Hold Advertising works with businesses to maximise their interaction with callers through professionally scripted, money-making on-hold marketing messages that turn callers into customers. We help businesses advertise to their most captive audience—their callers who are placed on hold. This is an amazing 70 per cent of callers, and they are put on hold for an average of 43 seconds. The name On Hold Advertising says it all, doesn't it?

Chapter 5

From imagination to...

setting goals for success

> High expectations are the key to everything.
>
> **Sam Walton**

Key points

- ¤ Create your business goals around your life goals, not the other way around.

- ¤ Use your goals to provide direction and motivation.

- ¤ Write down your goals or use pictures to remind you. Look at these every day.

- ¤ After you have set your goals, decide *how* you are going to reach them.

You have your idea, you've found your USP and named your business. What now? In this chapter we are going to look at setting goals, both for your personal life and for your business. Setting goals is an essential step towards running a successful business, no matter what type of operation it is. You will not know where you are going without them and you will have no way to measure success—although measuring a lack of success will still be possible. It happens when your bank account reads $0.00, or even worse, a big number with a minus sign in front of it.

Planning versus goals

Let's first address the difference between plans and goals, as many people confuse the two. Let's say in your first year of business you want to do the following:

- ¤ Make a profit of $150 000.

- ¤ Find 20 regular clients.

- ¤ Start a newsletter.

- ¤ Start a database of potential clients.

- ¤ Add two new services.

- ¤ Start a customer service telephone hotline.

- ¤ Hire two new staff members.

Is this a plan? No, it's not—though many budding entrepreneurs think it is. This is not a plan because it doesn't say anything about *how* you are going to do these things. These are goals.

Imagine you are about to go on holiday to Airlie Beach and you've never been there before. You've loaded up the car with towels, summer clothes, a frisbee, some zinc cream and the dog. No work for two weeks! Your partner jumps behind the wheel and gives you a big, excited hug, and says, 'Right, so how do we get there?' And you say, 'Airlie Beach'. That's what you are doing if you have goals but no plan. In this chapter we are going to look at setting goals. Creating a business plan is the subject of the next chapter.

Why are you going into business?

Before you go any further, you must decide *why* you are going into business. Put this book down for a few minutes and think about it right now—it's important! Before you even consider setting goals, such as profit or sales targets, you must know what you hope to achieve with your business as a whole. Do you want to be your own boss? Do you want to work fewer hours? Or more? Do you want more variety in your job? Or to travel as part of work? Do you want to start a business with your partner? You must be able to clearly state what your personal goals are, so that you can structure your business and create systems to meet them.

Many people don't think about this before getting started. They simply plan the business around their *business* goals and then once they are up and running they find that they are working more hours than they did in the past, when they really wanted to work less. Or they hire staff to keep up with demand, when they really wanted to work by themselves. This is a result of putting the business ahead of personal aims. And it's a mistake! Your business should be structured to meet your life goals, not your profit targets. Sure, profits are important, but are you going into business *just* to make money, or to improve the overall quality of your life?

You can set your own personal goals and desires for your business and then build a successful operation around these. Believe me, I know. I've done it—more than once! Don't be lulled into going with the conventional wisdom, such as you need to work nine to five, or you need to have lots of stock in a warehouse, or you need to spend lots of money to get started, or you need to hire lots of staff. Build your business how *you* want. Create *your own* business goals. For me, this is the essence of being an entrepreneur—and most people get it wrong! They never think about escaping conventions. If you are going to keep playing by everybody else's rules, why start your own business?

For example, if your goal is to create a business that allows you to travel, you can use the internet as your main distribution channel, arrange to have your products drop-shipped automatically when an order is placed, and conduct most of your customer service via email. Then you could be on safari in Africa, or at the top of the Eiffel Tower, or watching the sun set on the Gold Coast, and still be running your business (as long as you can access the internet!).

This isn't a traditional business model, but I've seen people have great success doing this.

Maybe your goal is to work fewer hours. You need to create business systems that don't require you to be constantly available during normal business hours. How do you do that? Outsource your customer service; automate your ordering and shipment; only take appointments in the morning; sell a product rather than offering a service. Or maybe your goal is to work *more* hours (perhaps the kids are driving you crazy), so you need to create business systems that will allow you to do this. Figure out what motivates you, what you are striving for, and then build your systems around this. We'll go into systems in more depth in chapter 7.

You must set both personal and business goals to be a successful entrepreneur. You will need the personal goals to help you when the going gets tough. If you have to work late or on the weekend while your friends go to the pub, or if that crucial order is accidentally sent to Siberia (again), you're going to have to remind yourself why you are doing this. And you need the business goals so that you—and others in your business—know where you are headed, and you will know when you get there.

Only when you have established your lifestyle goals for the business should you get down to the detailed stuff, such as profit levels, number of customers and inventory turnover. All of these goals should be considered secondary to your primary aim of building your business how you want it. Think about what targets you want your business to reach. Do some research. Find out what similar businesses earn, how many customers they have and what their profit percentage is. Also use your own experience if you are familiar with the industry.

Pete's tip: do it your way

I cannot emphasise this point enough. It's your business—do it your way. Being an entrepreneur is about fitting your business into your lifestyle, not the other way around. Only when you have established what your overall goals are for the business should you start worrying about goals such as profit targets.

One of the simplest ways to set goals for your business is to ask yourself some questions:

- How much do I want to earn?

- How many customers do I want?

- What percentage profit do I want to achieve?

- How many customers do I want to have in five years' time?

- How big do I want the business to be in five years' time?

- How many products do I want to sell this year? And next year?

- How many products do I want to have after five years?

You can see that you can set goals for just about anything. You must create goals that will take your business in a positive direction and make it strong. Once you have answered these questions you are well on the way to setting goals for your business.

> Obstacles are things a person sees when he takes his eyes off his goal.
>
> **E Joseph Cossman — entrepreneur**

How will you measure your goals?

Think about how you are going to measure your goals. Having a goal of 'making a large profit' is a good start, but what constitutes a large profit? Is $100 000 large, or $500 000? If you make a loss one year, a $100 profit will seem large. 'Large' is not quantifiable, so you will not know whether your goal has been reached. Make your goals measurable and specific, and set deadlines as well. 'Making a large profit' has no time line, so it will not encourage action. 'I want to lose weight' is not a useful goal either. Your goals *must* be tangible and measurable. Something that can't be quantified can easily be 'adjusted' and manipulated with hindsight, so in the end you can justify not achieving what you truly set out to do.

Here are some business goals you might set, that are measurable and have a time line:

- We will make $100 000 profit next year.

- We will sign up five new clients per month.

- We will introduce three new products next year.

Some measurable personal goals are:

- I will save $10 000 by 1 June next year so that I can go to Italy.

- I will cut down to five cigarettes a week in three months and quit completely two months after that.

- I will be able to run five kilometres without stopping by 31 December.

You can set goals over different time frames; for example, short, medium and long term. A short-term goal might be to finish by the end of the week that project that won't seem to go away . A medium-term aim might be to sign up a particular client by the end of next month. And your long-term goal could be to reach a certain financial target in two years.

You must be able to measure your goals as you go so that you can see whether you are on track or not. If your aim is to sign up 100 new clients in a year, don't wait until 26 December to find out you are only up to 17. Instead, see how many clients you have signed up after each fortnight or month and project this over the year. If you are falling behind 8.3 clients per month, this will alert you so that you can do something about it.

Pete's tip: make your goals measurable

Unquantified goals are never achieved.

Is it achievable?

Your goals are meant to provide you with motivation, so they should be challenging but achievable. If you can currently run 10 kilometres, having a goal to run 30 kilometres by next month is not realistic, but running 14 kilometres is. If your business made $60 000 this year, a target of $500 000 next year is probably not achievable, but $100 000 might be.

If your goals are unrealistic they will have the opposite effect, causing you to lose motivation as you realise that you are not going to reach your target and therefore give up. Set goals that will require you to work hard to reach them, but are still achievable. Likewise, a goal that is too easy to reach will be of little benefit. If you made $60 000 this year, a goal of $65 000 next year is not going to push you to get the most out of the business.

Having said that, though, *dream big*—if someone else has achieved something you want to achieve, there is absolutely no reason why you can't, too. All you have to do is model your actions on someone who has achieved something similar and you can get there. I truly believe that if somebody has already done something, then you can as well. There is no reason I will accept as to why you can't fly a plane, be a movie star, create a company that goes public, change the world ... we are all humans and if someone else has done it, then I ask you to justify why you couldn't—I bet you truly can't. The people who achieve these things were once just like you—sitting around with a good idea, wondering what to do with it.

> **Pete's tip: read your goals every day**
> *Write your goals down and stick the piece of paper on the fridge or your bedroom mirror, or beside your bed. Read them every day to remind yourself what you are working towards. This will give you motivation.*

> The big secret in life is that there is no big secret. Whatever your goal, you can get there if you're willing to work.
>
> **Oprah Winfrey**

Have you written it down?

Writing down both your business and personal goals will have a dramatic impact on whether you reach them. You can write them in your diary, or on a piece of paper and stick it on the wall. If your business goal is $100 000 profit, you can even place a graph on the wall of your office showing how you are progressing. Update it every fortnight. The constant reminder will motivate you to reach your goal and provide encouragement when you need it.

Pete's tip: don't just plan for the best

When planning and setting goals, consider what problems might arise. Consider the negative possibilities before you get underway, so that you are prepared when trouble comes.

You can also use images. If your goal is a trip to France, cut out a picture of the Eiffel Tower. If you are saving for a new car, put a picture of the car on your fridge, or set it as the wallpaper on your computer, or carry it in your purse or wallet so that you can pull it out at any time and look at it. This can be especially handy if you are trying to save money. Tempted by those new clothes that you don't really need? Pull out the picture of that red BMW that you drive in your dreams and this will motivate you to save the money for the car rather than spend it on the clothes.

A neat trick if you have to drive in peak hour to a crummy job every day, is to put your written goals on the back of your rear-view mirror and read them while you are stuck in traffic jams. Also, if this is the case and you have to spend lots of time in your car, either to get to the office or from meeting to meeting, forget the radio and invest in educational audio programs that will inspire and educate you. There are audio programs on every topic—from weight loss, to internet marketing, to copywriting.

Also, write down the benefits you will achieve from reaching your goals. For example, 'When I have quit smoking, I will be healthier, I won't have to go outside in the cold to smoke and I will save money.' Or, 'When I've saved the money for my trip, I'll be able to see the Mona Lisa, which is my favourite painting.'

I have a daily planner that I complete every night before I go to bed. It lists the top four goals that I am working on at that time, and the action I will take the next day to get closer to each of those goals. The next night I mark off whether that item was done or not. I also include a business associate I will call and touch base with, to see what they are up to and see what I can do to support them. It's amazing what can be achieved with a simple conversation. These are my business goals. I also have personal goals. My friends mean the world to me and, due to my busy schedule I don't get to party with them as much as I would like, so I include one friend I will call the next day to simply have a chat. I also have daily exercise goals.

I've included a copy of my planner (overleaf) to help you start planning for success.

Download:

My planner is included here. If you wish to download a free template that you can print out as many times as you like and use yourself, go to: <www.preneurmarketing. com.au/goalplanner.php>. There is also room in your From Imagination to Implementation Workbook *for you to write down your business goals.*

Daily Success Planner

Date: _____

Current goals:

1 _____

2 _____

3 _____

4 _____

What will I do tomorrow to get me closer to each goal?

1 _____ ❏ DONE

2 _____ ❏ DONE

3 _____ ❏ DONE

4 _____ ❏ DONE

Tomorrow's 'friend' contact: _____ ❏ DONE

Tomorrow's 'business' contact: _____ ❏ DONE

Today's checklist:

❏ Run a minimum of 5 km today

❏ Eat two pieces of fruit

❏ Repeat affirmations

❏ Do daily sit-ups

❏ Do daily push-ups

❏ Complete the Daily Success Planner

SIGNED: _____

Chapter 6

From imagination to...

planning the journey

The critical ingredient is getting off your butt and doing something.
It's as simple as that.

Nolan Bushnell — founder of Atari and Chuck E Cheese

Key points

¤ Use your business plan to work out where your business is now, where it is going and how it is going to get there.

¤ When preparing your plan, you might come across improvements you can make to your idea.

¤ Your plan will help you make decisions when you are up and running.

¤ A business plan can be used to present your business to potential investors or partners.

In this chapter we are going to look at planning; that is, how are you actually going to make all this happen? A business plan is an important part of business success. It will help you clarify what you are doing before you get started, and help you make decisions and define your direction when you are underway. It's about defining and gaining clarity for yourself more than anything and it will save you money through preparation. It is also useful to help explain your business to other people, such as potential investors or partners.

If you are anything like me, a stereotypical entrepreneur, you tend to want to jump in at the deep end and 'just do it', but a business plan is essential and will save you a lot of money (trust me). I am not talking a 104-page Harvard MBA–style plan; just a simple plan will make a world of difference to your venture.

You must make your plan realistic, otherwise it is of no use. This is not the place for marketing spin or outrageous sales predictions. Make it an informative, practical and well-thought-out document. Consider it a tool.

Your plan will tell you if your idea has legs and is viable. As many of us have experienced, others will have had a similar idea to the one you are about to take from imagination to implementation, and some research and a business plan will tell you if they were simply lazy and didn't act, or if the idea has no foundation and isn't worth pursuing. Your plan may also bring to light a completely new and more profitable way to go about things.

Never mistake activity for achievement.
John Wooden — great US college basketball coach

Your business plan

A business plan is often called a road map for your business and this is a good description. Without a plan, how will you know where you are going? How do you get to Airlie Beach if you have never been there before? As discussed in the previous chapter, don't confuse goals with a plan.

Your business plan will show where your business is now, where you want it to be in the future and — most importantly — how you are going to get there. It can be used to help you gain finance from a bank, to introduce new staff or investors to the business, and to give you and your staff direction. You can also use it to make business decisions and to assess them. As part of your plan you should be able to explain the reasoning behind the decisions you have made. If you are having trouble doing this in the plan, you might have made a poor or ill-informed decision.

A business plan is a working document. It should be updated when there is a major change in your business, such as a significant staff member leaves, a new product is introduced or a new source of finance becomes available.

Your business plan should include:

¤ a description of your business

¤ ownership details

¤ details of your product or service

¤ details of your customers and market

¤ details of the competition

¤ marketing details

¤ personnel details

¤ financing details.

You can also include an executive summary, which provides an overview of all of the above for quick reference. I will now look at each of these topics individually.

A description of your business

Your business plan must include all the boring details, such as:

¤ whether you are trading as a sole trader, partnership or company (discussed in chapter 9)

¤ the location of your business

¤ contact details

¤ when the business was formed

¤ the names of the people involved and what their roles are

¤ business registrations.

You can also include your vision or mission statement if you have one. This section should also include an overview of the business, such as the different departments and how they fit together.

I can't walk past a fat and complacent business sector without wanting to shake it up a bit.
Richard Branson

Ownership details

The ownership section should outline all parties that have an interest in the business and the form and size of that interest. It should also outline how profits and losses will be distributed, how each owner may be involved in the day-to-day running of the business and how ownership can be transferred. Also, make sure you clearly define any 'out clauses', in case a partner wants to leave the enterprise at some point; consensus upfront will save hundreds of headaches later on.

Details of your product or service

Your business plan must include a detailed description (and pictures, if appropriate) of the products or services that you are selling and why you believe they will be successful. This allows you to consider every aspect of what you are offering. Depending on your business, you should consider questions such as:

¤ How is the product going to be manufactured?

¤ Where will it be manufactured?

¤ How much will it cost to build and transport?

¤ How will stock be managed?

¤ How will we provide service to our customers?

¤ Who is going to provide the service?

¤ What will the recommended retail price be?

You should also describe the benefits of your products or services; that is, how they will help the people who use them. This sounds a lot like your unique selling proposition, doesn't it? Surprising? Not really! Also include here details of any patents you may have in relation to your products or services.

Details of your customers and market

It is essential to your success that you analyse who your target customers are. This can include details such

Pete's tip: update your plan

Update your plan whenever your business circumstances change, such as if you add a new manager or stop selling a product.

as where they live, what their average income is, what products or services they currently buy, how old they are and what might persuade them to use your business. You can obtain this data by doing your own market research or you may be able to buy the information from a marketing company. The Australian Bureau of Statistics may even have some research that will be helpful to you. This information will be further expanded on in your marketing plan.

Defining your typical/ideal customer early will give you enormous power when designing your marketing material later on, as you can get inside your customers' heads and work out what will appeal to them and get their attention.

Details of the competition

You must find out who your competition is and what they are offering. This is very easy — simply buy their products or use their services. Analyse their strengths and weaknesses and how their offerings compare to yours. Look at prices, how they advertise and who buys from them. Include the most important of these details in your plan. This is also where you can outline your unique selling proposition: what separates you from them? You must be able to clearly identify why you are an orange hanging on an apple tree!

Marketing details

You should have a separate, and much more detailed, marketing plan, but you can include here a summary of your marketing approach. Incorporate details of planned advertising, how the internet will be used, special promotions and sales.

Pete's tip: do your homework

Don't fill your business plan with assumptions and guesses. Do your homework and get all the figures, statistics and information you need to make your plan a meaningful and useful document.

This is one of the areas where you turn your goals into a plan. For example, your goal might be to increase sales by 10 per cent next year. As part of your business plan, this becomes, 'We will improve sales by 10 per cent next year by offering a discount for regular clients'.

Personnel details

List all the people who will be involved in the business, and clearly outline what each person's role is. Describe their skills, background and relevant experience, and why each person was chosen for each particular role. Include how long they have been with the company. Make sure you update this when there are any staff changes. This should also include the details of any people involved outside the company, such as accountants and lawyers. Also, include the people you are going to outsource jobs to and what criteria they must meet to qualify for this outsourced role. This will work as a reference tool when looking to replace people in the future.

Financing details

Describe how your business is going to be funded and how the finances will be managed. Have you taken out a loan to start the business? Do you have shareholders? Do you have an internal bookkeeper, or is this outsourced? How, and how often, are staff paid? Will money be borrowed in the future? And if so, for what purposes? What happens if there is a cash flow problem? How will the financial performance of the business be assessed?

This is not the place for detailed balance sheets or cash flow statements, it is more an overview of your business's approach to finance. It should contain historical and current information. You can also include financing projections in this section. This can cover what your financial goals are and how these were arrived at, and how the money will be used.

There is nothing more frightful than ignorance in action.
Johann Wolfgang von Goethe

$ $ $ $ $

Use your goals and plans to motivate yourself and others who are involved in your business. Set your goals high, to provide a challenge, and use your business plan to help you get there. Don't expect to reach your goals just because you have set them.

Chapter 7

From imagination to...

profitable systems

There are plenty of ways to get ahead. The first is so basic I'm
almost embarrassed to say it: spend less than you earn.

Paul Clitheroe

Key points

¤   Structure your business systems to meet your goals.

¤   Leverage your finances as much as possible to maximise
    profits and cash flow.

¤   Don't spend time on the menial parts of your business — pay
    other people to do this for you and use your own time more
    profitably.

Match your systems to your goals

One of the reasons for setting goals is to establish a direction. In
this chapter we are going to look at how to construct your business
systems so that they meet the goals you outlined in chapter 5. For
example, if one of your goals is to only work part-time, one of your
business systems might be to outsource some of the work. If one of

your goals is to be able to work from anywhere in the world, then your systems might be based around the internet.

There is no one perfect way to structure, or run, a business. You must create business systems that meet your unique business and personal needs. It's your business, so do it your way. Think about your goals and what you want from your business and life. If you wrote down your goals in your *From Imagination to Implementation Workbook*, read over them now before reading on.

What are *systems*?

My definition of a 'system' is:

Save

Your

Self

Time

Energy and

Money

Your business systems are the practical, nuts and bolts aspects of how your business is structured and run. But they are also more than this; good business systems will save you time, energy and money, and help you meet your goals. They will allow you to leverage your business for maximum profit.

> 94% of failure is a result of the system ... not people.
> **Edward Demming**

Leveraging your time and money

Take a bird's-eye view of your business structure, and see if you are operating in a way that meets your goals and also maximises your time and cash resources. It's all about *leverage*—making the most of every system and resource that you have available to you. In *The One Minute Millionaire*, Mark Victor Hansen and Robert G Allen outline five types of leverage:

- ¤ Other people's money — for example, taking out a bank loan leverages your money because you might be able to spend $100 000 while only putting up $20 000 of your own (but, of course, you have to pay it back later).

- ¤ Other people's experience — find a business mentor, read books, listen to audio programs, attend seminars — use any method you can to learn from people who have already been there and made the mistakes you are hoping to avoid.

- ¤ Other people's ideas — we've already addressed this in an earlier chapter — adapt an existing idea to create your own business.

- ¤ Other people's time — pay other people to do the 'grunt' work, such as making deliveries or constructing frames.

- ¤ Other people's work — many people simply want to earn a living — hire staff and pay them to do the everyday tasks in your business.

Hansen and Allen state that millionaires 'are masters at using all five kinds of leverage'. All types of leverage have the same ultimate goal — to increase *your* profits. Use your money, time and effort as wisely as possible.

For example, when selling the 'G, I could have easily made and delivered the frames myself. That's the obvious path to take in business; for instance, most apprentice plumbers start their own plumbing business and pick up the tools themselves. However, I decided from day one to structure my business so that I didn't do anything myself except planning, strategic thinking and — the most important aspect — sales. I consciously took less cash profit from the deal by outsourcing stuff like couriers and framing. For example, if I spent an hour making a frame and saved $80 that's a potential opportunity cost of two additional sales I could have made if I focused on sales and business strategies instead. Also, I would not have been as open to the other entrepreneurial opportunities that presented themselves because I would have been stuck in the shed with a hammer and glue. This means that saving that $80 would have ended up costing me a lot more in the long run. And why spend an hour delivering something that I can pay a courier $20 to deliver for me? Doing it myself actually ends up costing me money because I might have been able to generate sales worth $300 in that hour I spent driving to Dandenong. Paying other people to take on tasks for you, so that you can spend your time on more important things, is leveraging your time, and it is a vital ingredient for success. You limit the potential of your business if you do all the work yourself.

Pete's tip: leverage

Leverage both your time and money to maximise profits. Time and money are better spent generating more sales, not on the mundane tasks that you can pay somebody else to do for you. If you are the brains of the operation, don't spend your time packing boxes or licking stamps.

I would also prefer to make $1 as passively as possible rather than $2 working my arse off. Think about the bigger picture — you may make more money fixing toilets or painting houses yourself, but you will not have time to enjoy the money because you have structured the business so that you only get paid when you are using your own elbow grease — that's trading time for money. I would rather trade thoughts and ideas for money, as ideas and thoughts keep coming. Time is something you can never get back. This is why one of my goals for all my business ventures is to make as much money as possible while keeping the demands on my time to a minimum. You can do this too if you keep your goals in mind when setting up your business.

Leverage other people's skills and ideas. If you have a great idea for an internet business but still have trouble working a push-button phone, what's the point in doing a computer course and attempting to set up a website yourself? Simply find somebody who has the skills and pay them to set up your website, while you concentrate on the business side of things.

Creating your systems to meet your goals

It is one of my strongest beliefs that in business you should do it *your way*. Too many people start a business by copying whatever similar businesses are doing. Sure, this may seem safer, but will this allow you to meet *your* goals? And think about this: if you set your business up the same as everybody else, how do you expect to do better than them? How will you dominate your industry if you are doing the same things as everybody else? If nothing makes you stand out from the crowd, why will people pick you over your competitors? There is a difference between researching an industry and designing a business, and simply picking an industry and starting a business.

With this in mind, let's have a look at some examples of how to arrange your business systems (remember, Save Your Self Time, Energy and Money). Given the almost limitless types of businesses out there, I will not be able to examine every possible operation, but the following should give you an idea of how to match your systems to your goals.

Income before expenses—leveraging your money

The basic idea behind most businesses that sell products is to turn cash into stock, and then turn that stock back into cash as soon as possible. For example, a footwear store will have capital (cash), and purchase shoes (stock) to sit in the stockroom and on the shelves with the aim of selling the stock at a profit as quickly as possible. A whitegoods store pays up-front for the items in its showroom and then aims to generate a profit by selling these items to customers at a higher price. Toy stores stock toys that they have already paid for; bookshops stock books that they have already paid for; even restaurants have to pay for food and other ingredients that they then sell to customers as meals.

You should already have noticed the major drawback of running your business this way. Think of the amount of cash that is tied up in stock not earning you any money! If you are opening a bookshop, you might have to spend $150 000 just to put books on the shelf. And you will have to pay for most of these before you have made a single sale. It will take a long time to sell these books and recoup that cash and you know that some of the books simply won't sell, so this is cash that you will never get back. (Yes, there may be consignment or sale and return, but you get the idea.) The cash that has gone into buying this stock could have been used on marketing to generate further sales.

A few years back I considered purchasing an Athlete's Foot franchise. One of the reasons I didn't go ahead was the amount of stock I needed to purchase to be operational—it was a large investment. Even though I could have designed the business to meet my goal and had less stock, you need to be intelligent and still keep your customers in mind. Footwear buyers in a retail environment don't want to wait for their shoes to arrive; they will just go somewhere else and purchase them. Even though I am telling you to design it your way, you still need to be intelligent and consider your customer's objectives. You must design your business to suit your goals, but you must make sure your goals make business sense as well.

Becoming wealthy is not a matter of how much you earn, who your parents are, or what you do ... it is a matter of managing your money properly.
Noel Whittaker

One of my business goals is to limit the amount of capital I outlay initially, so I have come up with a better idea for a business model. What if your structure is to turn cash into cash, and then turn part of that cash into stock? 'Huh?' I hear you say. Let me explain. You will have some initial cash outlay when starting your business, no matter what you are trying to do. Why not focus your spending on getting the orders in? Set up a website and use publicity and advertising to attract traffic to your site. Then structure your ordering system so that you sell something and get paid up-front (turning cash into more cash), and then use part of this income to pay for the item you sold. This involves the same steps as the traditional model above, just in a different order. It minimises your capital requirements and maximises your cash flow. For example, if you want to open a bookshop, open it online, and instead of stocking the books, simply order them from the publisher when they are purchased from your site.

Cash flow is not just about how much money is going in and out of your business; equally important is *when* the money arrives or is spent. If you use the traditional business model described earlier, it is highly likely that you will have to pay for your stock before you have received money from your customers for those items—because your customers haven't bought from you yet! You might purchase $50 000 worth of stock that you are confident you can sell for $90 000. But what if your stock moves more slowly than expected, people are late paying their bills (it does happen regularly) and your supplier, accompanied by two large men, both named Brutis, comes knocking on your door at two o'clock in the morning asking for his money, but you don't have the cash—what happens then? Do you think he will be mollified by the fact that, when you have sold all of your stock, you will be able to pay him? Of course not. Your supplier has his own bills to pay. He wants his money.

> **Pete's tip: income before expenses**
>
> *Structure your business so that you collect money from your customers before you have to pay your suppliers for the item. This maximises your cash flow and avoids you having cash tied up in stock that is idle.*

In his blog on 'bootstrapping' (being a budding entrepreneur without much money), business author Guy Kawasaki says that if you are an entrepreneur but are short of start-up cash, you should:

> Start a business with a small up-front capital requirement, short sales cycles, short payment terms, and recurring revenue. It means passing up the big sales that take twelve months to close, deliver, and collect. Cash is not only king, it's queen and prince too ...

Kawasaki also suggests going direct to your clients, and understaffing at start-up to save costs. (This is a great blog about getting started with little money. Go to <blog.guykawasaki. com/2006/01/the_art_of_boot.html>.)

Do not underestimate how important cash flow is. Many businesses that have got off to a strong start, and appeared to be making profits, have gone under when they encountered cash flow problems. Poorly managed cash flow contributed to the collapse of One.Tel, which had signed up thousands of new customers to its services but was still spending money more quickly than it was coming in.

I resolved to stop accumulating and begin the infinitely more
serious and difficult task of wise distribution.

Andrew Carnegie — American businessman and philanthropist

Getting the income in before you incur the expenses has a few very important advantages:

- Your cash flow is increased because you don't have capital tied up in unsold items that have cost you cash but have not yet generated a return.

- It allows you to start your business with a small amount of capital, because there is no large initial outlay to purchase stock.

- You do not need to store your products, saving you warehousing expenses.

- You only buy or create the item when an order has been placed for it, so you don't end up with unsold stock sitting in a warehouse.

This is the system I used when I was selling the 'G. I set up the website, and of course I had to buy the carpet and the wood, but the frames weren't constructed until I received orders for them. This means I didn't spend a lot of money having 500 frames made up in one go only to leave them sitting in a storeroom while I went out and tried to sell them. Stock sitting idle ties up cash that could be better used elsewhere—mostly, in attracting more sales!

For this system to work you must structure the business so that you receive payment before you have to ship the product. Require payment up-front, but allow a delivery period. I advertised the frames with two weeks for delivery, giving us plenty of time to have the frame made and delivered *after* it had been ordered and paid for. I used some of the money that the customer had paid me to pay for the frame to be made. Structuring my business so that I could take orders prior to construction allowed me to get started with a small capital outlay and maximise my cash flow. I was not required to have huge stockpiles of frames already made, which would have restricted my cash flow rather, I worked on a make-to-order basis.

Think carefully, though, about whether this will suit your business—if your customers expect quick delivery, this system will not work. A two-week delivery is fine for something people are going to hang on the wall, but if you are selling building supplies, for example, this will most likely be unacceptable. Again, keep your business goals in mind. There's a fine line between getting paid before you produce a product and selling something that doesn't exist, so do your homework.

> What good is money if you can't inspire terror in your fellow man?
>
> **C Montgomery Burns**

Another way to structure your business so that you receive the income before paying out the cash is to develop a drop-shipping model. For example, if you are going to supply printer cartridges, instead of buying stock in bulk from your suppliers, hiring a warehouse and stocking 1373 different types of cartridges, why not work out a deal with your suppliers where they send out the orders for you, after you have received payment? This is called 'drop shipping'.

You may be able to make arrangements directly with the manufacturer, but if not, you will have to locate a wholesaler or distributor. You could take the orders and payments through your website and forward the orders directly to the relevant supplier for shipment. If the wholesale price of a particular cartridge is $75 plus $10 delivery and you sell it on your website for $125 plus $10 delivery, you will make $50 for each sale. You've avoided the costs of buying stock in bulk and storing it, and the hassle of sending the item out. Your supplier is also making a profit on the orders, and the customer will not know that you never actually stocked the item that he or she ordered from your company.

When picking suppliers to drop ship for you, make sure that they can meet your terms. If you promise customers delivery in three days, all of your suppliers must be able to do this. You must also investigate how the product is packaged when it is sent out, and what the company's sales and returns policies are. Remember, when the product arrives at your customer's doorstep, it has been purchased from *your* company and any problems will reflect badly on you, not the supplier. Your customer won't care who actually sent the product when he or she has to open the box with a crow bar and destroys the cartridge while doing so. The cartridge was purchased from your site and it is your responsibility to ensure your customers' needs are met.

Consider whether your business goals make this an appropriate business structure. If one of your goals is to have the largest range of products for people to browse, this obviously won't work because you'll have no stock! However, if one of your goals is to offer a huge range but have minimal capital outlay, drop shipping could be just right.

Pete's tip: investigate

Make sure you check out a manufacturer or supplier before making a drop-shipment deal with them. Your customers don't care who sent the product, and any problems will reflect badly on your business.

An added bonus of a drop-shipping business is that you can quickly change the products you are offering. If you decide at short notice that you wish to add a new product to your website, simply contact your supplier to make sure it's available and away you go. No need to order the stock and wait two weeks for it to arrive. It is also beneficial if a product is not selling well. No need to return unwanted stock to the supplier (if this is even possible), or sell remaining stock at below cost just to get rid of it. Simply take it off your website—problem solved.

Online auction site eBay is a perfect distribution channel for a drop-shipping business—you can sell just about anything on eBay and make arrangements with a manufacturer or distributor to send the product out for you. There are plenty of people these days who make a living by selling items over eBay. The other option is to base your business around your own website.

Outsourcing the work—leveraging your time

My latest business venture is On Hold Advertising <www.onhold advertising.com.au>. As explained earlier, I turn my clients' callers into customers with tailored on-hold marketing messages. I work with clients to get inside their business to uncover what should be communicated via their on-hold messages to ensure their callers are kept happy, educated and up-sold. I professionally script, record and produce a message that cross-promotes my clients' products and services, and provide industry-leading state-of-the-art equipment that is required to play the messages through the phone system 24/7. Except that I *don't actually do any of these things.*

Here's what really happens. When I receive an order for an on-hold marketing message system, I outsource the production work to Australia's leading production company, who I partner closely with. On Hold Advertising holds no stock and has no direct staff—the production company employs the scriptwriters and voice-over artists. On Hold Advertising is, fundamentally, a sales and lead-generation company. This business structure meets two of my key businesses goals—it minimises both the demands on my time and my capital outlay. I don't have to do the grunt work or be location specific, and I don't have to hold stock (equipment) or deal with staff. This allows me to focus on the money-making activities of a business and leverage my skill-set. I don't have to get bogged down with the hassle of staff politics, large overheads or technical stuff with clients; I simply focus on sales and marketing—the more enjoyable aspects of business. Think about it, what is more liberating and rewarding?

To minimise the amount of time you spend working in your business, and when you are working you want to use the time as profitably as possible, outsource as much of the work as you can. If you are starting a courier business, do you need to buy lots of vans or would you be better off using contractors and just running the booking system? In the case of starting a marketing company there are plenty of people you could outsource some of the work to. Find other businesses that can take on some of the work for you.

On the other hand, if the kids are running wild or your mother-in-law lives in a granny flat out the back of your place and she drives you crazy, maybe you want to do it all yourself and work as much as you can. It's about doing it your way!

Selling your time will never make you rich. You must always develop systems and use someone else's time to produce something you can sell at a higher price.
Brian Sher — author of *What Rich People Know & Desperately Want to Keep a Secret*

Other systems

One aspect that people seldom give much thought to is their opening hours. Do you need to be open from 9 am to 5 pm? If one of your goals is not to have to work full-time or to have to work standard hours, why structure your business this way? If you want to be finished for the day when the kids come home from school, why not work from 8.00 am to 3.30 pm? It doesn't matter that those aren't standard hours. People can email you or leave you a message and you can get back to them the next morning.

> **Pete's tip:**
> **do it your way**
> *Don't just blindly copy an existing business structure. Build your business so that it meets your unique business and personal goals. It's your business!*

It's a common misconception that you need to be constantly available. I think there can be value in making yourself a little hard to reach. Your customers will think you are always busy and in demand, and they will feel lucky when they get through to you. Do you expect to be able to get the prime minister on the phone? Or the head of one of the big banks? Or the boss of Telstra? Of course not. And did you ever hear about a wise man at the *bottom* of a mountain? Hugely successful marketing guru Dan Kennedy makes a conscious effort to be hard to get hold of. He does not take unscheduled phone calls or have email and the phones in his office will only be answered on Wednesday afternoon. How's that for exclusive?

There is a shoe store in New Zealand that will only see you if you make an appointment—yes, you can only buy a pair of shoes from this store if you make a prior appointment. The implication is that the staff will give you such good service you must book ahead. That's a great example of doing something a bit different to make the business stand out.

Workbook:
In your From Imagination to Implementation Workbook, *list five business systems that will help you reach your goals.*

How are you going to communicate with your customers? If your goal is to be able to travel while you work, base your business around the internet. Set up a drop-shipment business that allows people to order and pay online and provide customer service via email. Automate an email marketing system—you can be running your business from the south of France and your customers will never know. On the other hand, if you think your biggest strength is your personal ability to sell your product or service, set up your business so that you are the person customers deal with and have other people manage the other parts of the business.

Do you need a meeting room or the appearance of a large office but don't want the expense, or you would rather work from home? How about using a virtual office? A virtual office is a business that will answer your phone for you as though it is your business, take messages, and receive faxes and mail. It may also have a meeting room you can book. All of this will help give the appearance of a large, bustling business while keeping your costs under control. Just type 'virtual office' into a search engine to see the options available.

Chapter 8

From imagination to...

pricing for profit

> Many companies act as though 100 per cent of the population is price-obsessed. This delusion nibbles away at their profits and attracts only the most disloyal of all customers.
>
> Jay Conrad Levinson — *Guerrilla Marketing*

Key points

¤ Price is about *value*—it's not about being 'cheap' or 'expensive'.

¤ There are various methods you can use to set prices, but ultimately the market will decide what you can charge.

¤ Keep in mind the type of business image you are trying to portray when setting your prices. Consider your pricing as part of your overall business strategy.

Pricing is often a difficult issue for budding entrepreneurs because if you get it wrong, it can be disastrous for your business. Too high and you won't make enough sales to generate the profit you require; too low and you will make lots of sales but not generate the profits you need. This can be especially difficult if you've come up with a completely new idea. Nobody has done this before, so how do you figure out what to charge for it? Pricing also helps to position your business in the market. For example, are you trying to position yourself as a low-price, no-frills operator, or a higher priced, top-quality business?

Price is about value and perception

Before we have a look at the different methods you can use to set a price, let's consider what makes a price the *right price* for a particular product or service.

Value

Get rid of the notions of 'cheap' and 'expensive'—price is about *value*. What is the product or service worth to the person buying it? If you saw a bottle of water for $15 in your local supermarket, there's no way you would buy it. But if you had just run a marathon and the only water available was selling for $15 a bottle, I bet you would be reaching for your cash. What about if you were looking to hire a lawyer? Nobody would pay top dollar for a fancy lawyer just to review a contract to buy a house, but what about if you were being sued for $2 million because your homemade chimney collapsed on your next-door neighbour's aviary of rare birds and killed everything inside? Suddenly, $400 an hour would seem quite reasonable. And why are the prices at the local 24-hour store higher than at the supermarket? Because when you run out of milk at 7 am, you don't care that you have to pay 75¢ extra for a litre—you just want your Coco Pops. Food and drink prices are higher at the football and other events because it's very inconvenient to leave the stadium to buy elsewhere—how's that for a captive market!

So how does this help you with pricing? The lesson is that the prices you can charge are directly related to how much people need or want your product. It's not simply a matter of saying, 'I want to make $5.00 for each widget we sell' or 'Each widget costs us $7.50 to manufacture, so let's sell them for $15.00'. You must give your customers value. If you don't, your desired profit margins and manufacturing costs won't matter a bit.

> If the only thing binding your customers to your company is the lowest price,
> your business will be as fragile in its tenth year as in its tenth week.
>
> **Dan Kennedy — *No B.S. Business Success***

Perception

The prices of your products or services should be considered as part of your overall business strategy. What you charge will affect how your business is perceived by customers. High prices imply high quality and exclusivity, while low prices can imply poor quality. Keep in mind your target market and your business goals when setting prices.

Once your business has built a good reputation, you will be able to increase prices. Companies that are considered prestigious are able to charge more for a product. I bet Porsche can charge at least 20 per cent more for its cars just because of its reputation. The same goes for makers of clothes and shoes. Nike, for example, can charge premium prices, as can Country Road. Starbucks sells coffee at a price higher than McDonald's or your local coffee shop. It can do this because of the brand it has established — it comes back to defining a USP and delivering on that. You can hang out in Starbucks on the comfy couches, listen to the music and drink the really good coffee — that's their point of difference.

Price perception also applies to individual products and services. There are many examples of a price hike actually *increasing* sales. I know of a men's clothing store that was having trouble moving a particular range of shirts for $29.95. The manager dropped the price to $19.95, but it didn't make much difference. So he increased the price to $39.95 — and suddenly the shirts started racing out the door! Why did this happen? Because at $19.95 the shirt is perceived as being cheap and people expect the quality to be poor. But at $39.95, people think they are buying a nice shirt. I know of a gentleman who was selling a car that had been left to him in a will. He knew nothing about cars and just wanted to get rid of it, so he advertised it for $10 000. Every person who enquired asked if it had been in an accident or if there was something else wrong with it. The car didn't sell. He thought this was interesting, so he increased the price to $16 000 — and the car sold the next day. The low price gave the impression that there was a problem with the car.

Pete's tip: people *will* pay

People will happily pay high prices for products that benefit them or provide them with something they desire. If they didn't, companies such as Porsche, Bang & Olufsen and Versace would not have survived.

The obvious lesson is that something can be priced too low, giving the perception that it's not very good. Customers will stay away. People expect to pay for good quality, so don't assume that simply dropping your prices will help to lift sales if things are moving slowly. We've already looked at finding a hungry market and identifying a unique selling proposition; if you've done these things well, there should be a high demand for your product and this will be reflected in the prices you can charge.

Different pricing methods

You've figured out what your product or service is and who you think is going to buy it, but how much are you going to charge for it? There are numerous ways you can work this out. See which of the following best suits your business and your market.

Compare your prices to the competition and to industry standards

Comparing your prices to those of the competition and to industry standards is one of the most common ways of setting prices, but it's not always the best. You should know what your competitors are charging and take this into consideration, but if you have come up with a good USP, you should be able to charge a little more.

It is very easy to see what current prices are — simply shop around. Surf the net, go to the local shopping centre, make a few phone calls. Consider what separates you from these other businesses and think about what this means for your pricing.

Calculate prices based on costs

Calculating prices based on costs is another common technique and is very simple. Add up all of your production costs and overheads and make sure you include all expenses (such as transport, wages, office running costs, retailer discounts, superannuation and insurance). If all of your expenses come to, for example, $3.00 per unit, and you wish to make $2.00 per unit sold, then your price will be $5.00 (or maybe $4.99).

Calculate 'backwards' based on how much profit you wish to earn

Calculating 'backwards' based on how much profit you wish to make is similar to the method above but you start at the other end and it is more useful for service businesses. If your goal is for your business to make $100 000 profit per year and you will work 2000 billable hours (40 hours per week for 50 weeks), work out how much you need to charge per hour to reach this goal.

Charge what you think your product or service is worth

Charging what you think your product or service is worth, while still taking into account some of the factors mentioned above, is another strategy you may employ. Do you think you can sell for $250 per unit while everybody else is selling at $220? Go for it! Just make sure you can clearly identify *why* you think your customers will pay more.

Charge what the market will bear

Charging what the market will bear is the final approach to pricing and will actually overrule all the others, whether you like it or not. No matter how you've arrived at your pricing structure, the test of whether you can sell at these prices will be the market — but remember that your positioning and USP determines your market.

Listen to the market

The only true test of whether you are selling at the right price is your customers. Once you are up and running, carefully study your sales patterns.

If your product moves slowly, maybe you're charging too much for it. Or, perhaps a better way to look at it is that your product or service is not attractive enough at this price. If sales are slow, don't automatically drop your prices. Competing on price can be dangerous to the health of your business, as it leaves you open to competition. Instead, consider what you can add to your product or service that will entice customers. Have another look at your USP; if sales aren't good, maybe your USP isn't as compelling as you thought, or it's not what your customers are after.

Pete's tip: don't be afraid to increase prices

People are often worried about increasing prices, but if you are very busy, then you most likely have room to raise your prices without losing business.

If your product is racing out the door faster than you ever hoped for, maybe you should be charging more. If you feel you have room to increase your prices, then do so. Your product or service is worth whatever people will pay for it and you are in business to make money. If the demand is there, take advantage of it. Your customers will quickly tell you if you've gone too high — they will stop opening their wallets and purses.

Another way to find out how much your customers expect to pay is to ask them. You can also get feedback from your staff or salespeople.

Other pricing ideas

Here are some other pricing ideas for you to consider. Keep in mind your target market and the goals of your business and don't be afraid to do something a bit different.

Prepayment

There are a number of industries for which the whole business model is built around prepayment for services, such as:

¤ Tanning salons—they encourage you to pre-purchase a book of 10 tanning vouchers, knowing that the majority of people will not use the entire book.

¤ The fitness industry—a friend of mine who runs a successful gym told me he 'banks' on people purchasing memberships and not actually attending the gym. If everyone who had a membership actually used it the recommended amount (three or four times a week), the gym wouldn't have enough equipment to accommodate them. (This isn't from a lack of trying on his behalf; he really wants to help people meet their weight and fitness goals and does everything he can to make his clients visit more often, but he is a realist and knows he needs that 'slack factor' to make his business profitable.)

As you have probably guessed by now, I am a big advocate of taking proven formulas from one business or industry and applying them to another. For example, McDonald's stole the drive-thru from the banking industry and look at the huge success they have had with it. So can your customers prepay for your product or service? For example, there is a tradesperson company in Queensland that pre-sells domestic labour. This company offers clients the ability to purchase 'ten quality tradesperson visits' a year for a set amount. The way it is pitched is that if you prepay you can call on them 24/7 and not pay any call-out fee or premium if you need to call a tradesperson out after hours.

There are many advantages in doing this:

¤ The main benefit for the handyperson is obvious—money up-front!

¤ The main benefit for the clients is again obvious—it saves them money and headaches when they need a tradesperson.

¤ The clients have been locked in as customers who won't shop around because they've pre-purchased the service.

¤ The other benefit for the tradesperson — and what he or she is banking on — is that the customers may not use all of the vouchers, resulting in more profit.

Of course, for this to work it must also provide benefits to your customers. They will receive cheaper rates because they have paid up-front, and they won't have to shop around to find a tradesperson next time they need something done.

You can also upsell to customers who generally only make one booking at a time. For example, if your business is detailing cars, offer a package of four details in a year for $250, rather than the one-off price of $85.00.

Here's another example: I received a letter from my accountant offering 'audit protection'. It only costs $22 and will protect me for up to $1100 worth of costs if I am audited. This is a great example of an added service that can be pre-sold.

Prices are never set in stone, and consumers expect them to change with the times.
<www.entrepreneur.com>

Renting

Can your product be rented to your customers instead of sold? This will provide you with a steady income stream and a larger profit in the long run, and your customers will not have to make a single large payment. It is common for businesses to rent computer equipment and furniture for the tax benefits. One way I could have used this method in the MCG venture is if I'd made MCG frames available for corporations to rent and hang in their boardrooms. For example, I could have offered the frames for two years' rental to businesses for $25 per month. This would give me residual income over 24 months and a higher profit per frame. Plus, I would receive the frames back at the end of the rental period, to either rent out again or sell (probably at a reduced price). Hey, that's not a bad idea … Rebel Sport sells ski equipment and also offers it for hire. Remember, think differently. If a technique isn't common in your industry this doesn't mean you shouldn't use it — it's often the way to go.

Variable price structure

Can you offer different products or levels of service at different prices? An obvious example is a courier company that charges $30.00 for one-hour delivery, $17.50 for same-day delivery and $12.50 for overnight delivery. See if there is anything you can add or subtract to provide a different package at a different price, with the aim of attracting more customers to your business. When selling the 'G, as explained earlier, I offered a series of frames with the authentic MCG timber and a series with standard mahogany frames to cater for all budgets.

Perhaps you can offer a no-frills version of your product and sell it on the internet. Automate the payment and dispatch, set up a Google Adwords campaign and then you can forget about it. You should remove all the branding so that it doesn't interfere with the brand you are trying to build. By doing this you will receive extra income for minimal effort.

Free!

One price that always seems to be a winner is $0. Can you give something away to attract customers? For example, if you are going to sell microwave ovens for $500, offer a free set of microwave dishes valued at $75. Only offer this to the first 100 buyers to further encourage people. Or offer a bonus for a two-week period.

At the time of writing, Target is offering a bonus Disney DVD when you spend more than $45 on Disney DVDs. And Ford is offering a special Falcon package with a bonus six-stack CD player, alloy wheels, leather steering wheel and other free items. When selling the 'G, I gave away a free piece of the Ponsford Stand timber to the first fifty people who bought a frame.

Do your sums carefully, though. The loss from giving something away must be more than compensated for by the resultant increase in sales. The secret is to offer something that doesn't cost you much, but will have a high level of perceived value for the customer. Think about those potential customers who are leaning towards buying from you but just need an extra nudge. What can you offer that will push them over the edge to buy your item, or entice them away from the competition?

Another good way to use bonuses is to give away a gift voucher with each purchase, or to potential customers to encourage them to buy. For example, if you sell computer software, customers could receive a voucher for a box of blank CDs with their next purchase. Or set up a cross-promotion deal with a joint venture partner (see chapter 16); you give away one of its products and it gives away one of yours.

You can also offer something for free by providing a trial of your product. Whatever your product or service is, give people a free sample—a free manicure, a free car wash, a free shampoo sample or a free trial version of your software. This encourages potential customers to try your offerings and if they like it they are more likely to buy.

I think it's very important that whatever you're trying to make or sell ... has to be basically good. A bad product and you know what? You won't be here in ten years.
Martha Stewart

Loss leaders

A loss leader is when a business deliberately sells something at a loss to attract customers, with the aim of upselling them when they purchase. This is a very common tactic, especially in large department stores such as Target and Kmart. For example, a sporting goods store might sell soccer balls and basketballs at a loss to attract kids and feature these low prices in their advertising. This is done with the expectation that when the kids come in with their parents to purchase, they will also want to buy new boots, T-shirts and other items. Once again, you must do your sums carefully to make sure that the loss on the loss leaders is compensated for by the overall increase in profits. If you have an older product line that is starting to slow down, maybe this would make a good loss leader.

Wal-mart in the US actually built its business on this model. It would advertise a particular item, such as 'X Brand' microwaves, at a low price to get people to come into the store. As customers perused the cheap microwaves the clerks would go over the customers' needs with them. The majority of the time they were able to upsell the prospective buyer a higher priced unit. Customers had walked through the door expecting to purchase a microwave and also expected all the microwaves to be cheap. Once they realised that the advertised unit wouldn't meet their needs, they purchased one on the shelves that met their needs without shopping around on price. Rumour has it that quite often the non-advertised units were more expensive than the customer could have paid elsewhere, but they didn't due to the perception created by the loss leader.

Instalments

Can your customers pay you in instalments? Maybe for your higher priced products people could make three or four payments either before or after receiving the product. This will attract those who want to buy your products but don't want to make a single large cash payment.

For example, we've all seen the ads for 'ginzu knives' or the CD collections of 1960s and 1970s music — pay in six easy instalments! This allows the customer to spread the financial outlay and it also helps to make the item seem cheaper. The customer receives the goods immediately but pays over a period of time. Harvey Norman and other furniture outlets often sell on credit with 18 months interest free, which is also a form of paying in instalments.

Another way to structure this is to have people pay in instalments and receive the product when the full amount has been paid. For example, Chrisco sells Christmas hampers, toys and other items, but you pay for them during the year and receive them in December. This helps ease the financial burden for that time of the year.

Be careful though — you *must* have a system for checking the creditworthiness of your customers if you are going to provide credit. The odd customer who doesn't pay won't do too much damage, but it will certainly be a problem if it happens often. This is an even bigger risk for services businesses. If you have sold a product you can at least attempt to recover it if payment is not made, but if you have already performed a service, there's not much you can do. Maybe going to the client's house and bulldozing the garage you built will make you feel better, but it won't get you your money back (although sitting outside your client's house in a bulldozer with the engine running might be a good time to ask for payment).

Lay-by/lay-away

Lay-by is another way for people to pay off an item over time. The customer picks out a particular item and it is put aside for them until they pay in full. Lay-by may encourage your customers to purchase when they are looking at a particular item but do not have the cash at that time.

One option that enables your clients to pay over time, no matter what products you sell, is Layby.com <www.layby.com.au>. You can become a vendor on this site, and the Layby.com payment system allows your clients to pay in small amounts. Once they have paid the full amount, the vendor is notified, and when the product is dispatched, payment is released to the vendor.

Download:

In your From Imagination to Implementation Workbook, *write down two or three ways you could include each of these techniques in your business.*

Membership

Can you charge for membership to a club that gives the customer benefits or discounts? Often businesses give memberships away so that they can get names on a database and build loyalty (which I highly recommend), but you may be able to charge for this. For example, Qantas charges for membership to its club. Of course, if you are going to charge, you have to offer more than people would usually receive from a free club.

> The buyer decides if the price is acceptable by determining
> benefits and by considering the competition.
>
> **Ken Evoy — business author**

Adjusting your prices

You should always be careful when adjusting your prices, either up or down. Remember, the important thing is how much money you make, not how many items you sell. If you reduce your price, it is possible to sell more items but make less money. For example, if a vitamin company had a storewide margin of 25 per cent and had a 15 per cent sale, it would have to increase sales by 150 per cent to make the same profit. Of course, the main point of a sale is often to move stock and clear the shelves, but this should still be kept in mind.

Table 8.1 (developed by Shannon Curtis <www.profitable clothingretailer.com>), shows how much sales would have to increase for a given price reduction. For example, if your gross profit is 30 per cent and you reduce your prices by 10 per cent, you will have to increase sales by 50 per cent to earn the same amount of money. This is highlighted in table 8.1.

Table 8.1: gross profit versus discount reduction

Your gross profit	10	15	20	25	30	35	40	50	100
2	25%	15%	11%	9%	7%	6%	5%	4%	2%
3	43%	25%	18%	14%	11%	9%	8%	6%	3%
4	67%	36%	25%	19%	15%	13%	11%	9%	4%
5	100%	50%	33%	25%	20%	17%	14%	11%	5%
10		200%	100%	67%	50%	40%	33%	25%	11%
15			300%	150%	100%	75%	60%	43%	18%
20				400%	200%	133%	100%	67%	25%
25					500%	250%	167%	100%	33%

Discount reduction (row label)

Let's see what happens when prices are increased. If a footwear store is selling a shoe for $149.95, with a 30 per cent margin, and it increases the price by 10 per cent, it can afford to have a drop in sales of 25 per cent without losing any profit. This is highlighted in table 8.2.

This table shows how much of a percentage of your sales you can afford to lose for a given price increase and still make the same amount of money.

Table 8.2: gross profit versus price increase

Your gross profit		10	15	20	25	30	35	40	50	100
Increase	2	17%	12%	9%	7%	6%	5%	5%	4%	
	3	23%	17%	13%	11%	9%	8%	7%	6%	
	4	29%	21%	17%	14%	12%	10%	9%	7%	
	5	33%	25%	20%	17%	14%	12%	11%	9%	
	10	50%	40%	33%	29%	25%	22%	20%	17%	
	15	60%	50%	43%	37%	33%	30%	27%	23%	
	20									
	25									

Selling the 'G

Let's have a quick look at how some of these strategies could have been used for selling the 'G (keep in mind that, like all businesses, I could not initially implement every different pricing model in my business — but I've given myself something to think about writing this!):

¤ As mentioned, I could have rented the frames to businesses.

¤ I could have given away a laminated poster of the MCG with each sale, as a bonus.

¤ I could have sold laminated posters as loss leaders.

¤ I could easily have offered a lay-by or instalment system.

Use the pricing methods that are most appropriate to your business to begin with, and add others as you expand.

On Hold Advertising

At On Hold Advertising we offer the following pricing options:

¤ Instalment options for people who want to own the unit outright, as well as a rental package for people more focused on cash flow.

¤ We also sell other telco products as loss leaders to increase our prospects lists and identify people we can sell the on-hold solutions to.

¤ We even give auto-attendant messages free to certain buyers.

Chapter 9

From imagination to...

the technical stuff

> Genius is 1 per cent inspiration and 99 per cent perspiration. Accordingly a genius is often merely a talented person who has done all of his or her homework.
>
> **Thomas Edison**

Key points

¤ Choose your business structure carefully, as it will have a significant impact on the way your business is run and the costs involved.

¤ Talk to a lawyer or an accountant for help with the decisions in this chapter.

¤ Each state and territory has different requirements, so do your homework for your location.

In this chapter we are going to look at the housekeeping aspects of starting your business, such as choosing a business structure, registering a business name and registering for GST. No, this stuff is not as exciting as coming up with the great ideas, making sales, or undertaking a marketing campaign, but getting it right is just as important. There are certain registrations that are required for you to operate a business and the structure that you select for your business can have an effect on your profitability. You must also decide whether you need to register for GST and other tax requirements.

So let's get into it.

Choosing a business structure

The structure that you choose for your business will have an impact in a number of ways. It can affect:

¤ how much tax you pay

¤ how you pay yourself and any staff

¤ your legal obligations

¤ how much it costs you to start up and run your business

¤ how decisions are made in your business

¤ your personal responsibilities.

Make sure you fully investigate the options and the implications of each and make a decision that is appropriate to your business. There is no one set-up that is appropriate for all businesses—and it is up to you to make the right decision for your venture. An accountant or a lawyer will be able to provide you with useful advice for your specific circumstances. Also, investigate any legislation or requirements specific to your state or territory.

There are four types of structures commonly used by businesses in Australia:

> **Pete's tip: get help!**
>
> *I studied tax law at university, but I am far from being an expert or registered adviser. This chapter is designed only as a guide—please make sure you consult your lawyer and accountant when setting up and dealing with the technical stuff.*

¤ sole trader

¤ partnership

¤ company

¤ trusts.

Sole traders

A sole trader operates a business as an individual. There is no separate business entity and the person running the business is responsible for all decisions, holds all legal liability and owns all the profits and losses. Business assets are considered to belong to the individual.

This is the simplest way to operate a business. When you are operating as a sole trader, you do not need a separate tax file number for the business and you declare all income and losses in your personal tax return. You will, however, need to apply for an Australian Business Number (ABN), which you will be required to use in your business dealings. It is not necessary to have separate bank accounts to trade as a sole trader; however, I would still suggest opening business accounts as it makes it easier to keep track of your business income and expenses. You are not legally required to pay superannuation to yourself if you are a sole trader, but it is definitely a good idea to do so. Here are some of the advantages and disadvantages of being a sole trader.

Table 9.1: advantages and disadvantages of being a sole trader

Advantages	Disadvantages
Inexpensive to set up and run	Individual is solely responsible for running the business, which means it can be difficult to take holidays, and major problems can be caused with even a short break due to illness
No business registration required	
Individual has complete control	
No separate tax return or tax file number required	Individual holds personal legal liability for the business

Table 9.1 (cont'd): advantages and disadvantages of being a sole trader

Advantages	Disadvantages
Fewer reporting responsibilities	Tax paid on business earnings at individual tax rate
	Options for finance might be restricted as a sole trader is usually seen as a small operation

Partnerships

A partnership is where two or more people join together to run a business. As with a sole trader, there is no separate legal entity for the business, but the partnership will require its own tax file number and ABN, and a separate tax return must be lodged for the partnership. Partners can decide how profits will be shared—it does not have to be 50/50. If one partner is spending more time on the business, this person can receive a greater share of the profits. Business assets are considered to belong to the partners and a partner can be an individual or a company.

If you select this structure it is extremely important that you have a written agreement between all parties before commencing business. This should include details of:

¤   how profits *and losses* will be split between the partners

¤   each person's role in the business

¤   how disputes will be resolved

¤   how the finances of the business will be managed

¤   under what circumstances the partnership can be dissolved.

Even if you are starting up with your best friend or a family member, make sure you have an agreement in place. This doesn't necessarily mean that you are expecting problems down the track, it simply gives you a document to help you run your business and make decisions. You should have a lawyer help you draw up this agreement and have it signed by all partners.

Choose your partners carefully and look for people who have skills that complement yours. If you are good at marketing but not numbers, find a partner who is an accountant. If you are not an outgoing person but your business idea will depend a lot on building relationships with people, find a partner who is gregarious and friendly. A partnership formed just on friendship may not be the best way to go if you have not carefully considered what each partner brings to the business and wants out of it. Table 9.2 lists some of the advantages and disadvantages of partnerships.

Table 9.2: advantages and disadvantages of partnerships

Advantages	Disadvantages
Inexpensive to set up and run	Partners hold personal legal liability for the business
Having more than one person involved brings added expertise to the business	Tax is paid on business earnings at individual tax rates
Income can be split in any proportion between partners	There is the possibility of disputes arising between partners

Companies

If you create a company to operate your business, you are establishing a separate legal entity. This means that the company—not the individuals involved—owns the assets of the business, and the profits and losses. A company is owned by shareholders and is run by directors; it must have separate bank accounts, its own tax file number and ABN, and file its own tax return. At the time of writing, companies pay tax at the fixed company tax rate of 30 per cent, and the profits are retained within the business, to be spent or paid out either as salary or dividends.

A company structure limits the legal liability of the owners (which is especially handy if you are sued for any reason). This is one of the most common reasons for choosing this structure. In the unfortunate event of your business going bankrupt, creditors only have a legal claim over the assets of the business, in most circumstances. They will not be able to come after the family home, which could happen if you are trading as a sole trader and your business collapses.

The downside of setting up a company is that there are more legal, tax and administrative requirements, and you must pay to register your company. Companies must conform to the *Corporations Act 2001* and are regulated by the Australian Securities & Investments Commission (ASIC). This places heavy responsibility for the legal compliance of the business on the company directors (this will most likely mean you). The following table notes some of the advantages and disadvatages of forming a company.

Table 9.3: advantages and disadvantages of companies

Advantages	Disadvantages
Limited legal liability for the owners	More expensive to set up and run than other structures
Easy to transfer ownership through the sale of shares	More complex tax and reporting requirements, resulting in more time and money spent on administration
The business is less likely to rely on just one or two individuals	
Business income is taxed at the fixed company rate	More legal responsibilities than other structures
It can be easier to attract outside finance	

Doctors are the same as lawyers; the only difference is that lawyers merely rob you, whereas doctors rob you and kill you too.
Anton Chekhov

Trusts

The Australian Taxation Office (ATO) defines a trust as 'an obligation imposed on a person to hold property or income for the benefit of others (who are known as beneficiaries)'. A trust is most often used for tax-planning purposes and a common structure is the family trust. Of the four structures examined in this chapter, this is probably the least used for business.

A trust must have its own tax file number and ABN, and lodge a tax return. It is run by trustees, who must meet certain legal obligations in this role and who own the assets of the trust for the benefit of the beneficiaries. A trust is required to have a trust deed, which outlines who the trustees and beneficiaries are, how the trust will be run and how the money earned by the trust will be distributed. Table 9.4 shows some of the advantages and disadvantages of setting up a trust.

Table 9.4: advantages and disadvantages of trusts

Advantages	Disadvantages
Income can be distributed in different proportions to beneficiaries	Complicated to set up and run
	Complicated taxation requirements
Tax can legally be minimised in some circumstances	Can be difficult to get out of

Business registrations

You will be required to have various registrations to operate your business. These will depend on what structure you have chosen. Requirements also vary between states and territories, so make sure you check out what is required in your location.

Registering a business name

Unless you are simply going to trade under your own name, your business name must be registered. If you just add something to your name — such as Anna Clemann Photography — you still must register. But we have already discussed and created a compelling business name, right?

Business names are registered in the state where your head office is (unless you are a company) and costs around $100. Contact the relevant government department in your state to find out how to do this (simply type 'business name registration' and the state you are in into an internet search engine). You can usually register online, over the phone, or at the relevant offices. The government department will also have a facility for you to find out if the name you have chosen is already registered or if there is a name that is similar. (Make sure you check Australia-wide, as the state-based website might only provide details for that state. You should also check registered trademarks.)

Your business name should be registered in each state or territory you intend to operate in. If you are operating in only one state, but send products interstate or work with interstate clients, you are required to be registered only in the state in which you actually operate. Once your name is registered, it must be clearly displayed anywhere that your business operates, and it must also appear on all of your business stationery, invoices and receipts. A name is registered for three years and there will be a renewal fee at the end of this period.

It is very important to be aware that registering your business name does not necessarily provide legal protection for that name. The same name may be registered in another state or territory or it may be registered through ASIC. If you wish to ensure that your business name is legally protected, you should also register it as a trademark. This is done separately (go to <www.ipaustralia.gov.au>).

Workbook:

Choosing the right business structure is very important, so think about it carefully. Do your homework and get some advice. You can change your structure once you are up and running, but this will be costly and time consuming. To get started, in your From Imagination to Implementation Workbook *write down which business structure you think will be best for you, and explain your reasons.*

If you are trading as a company, your business name must be registered with ASIC. This is done as part of the company registration process and you do not need to register at the state level. If you have thought of a great name but are not quite ready to register your business, ASIC will hold that name for two months. Go to <www.asic.gov.au> for more information.

There are certain restrictions placed on the names that can be registered. Names that are considered offensive will not be approved and special permission must be obtained to use certain words, such as 'chartered', 'university' and 'building society'. Also, you cannot use a name that would suggest a link with the government.

> A jury consists of twelve persons chosen to decide who has the better lawyer.
>
> **Robert Frost**

Company registration

As mentioned, a company is an independent legal entity and must be registered with ASIC. This is valid throughout Australia — there is no need to register in each state or territory. At the time of writing, registration costs $800.

There are three ways to register your company:

¤ Your lawyer or accountant can do it for you.

¤ You can do it yourself through ASIC.

¤ You can buy a 'shelf company'. (These are company structures that are already set up, and ownership and all the necessary details will be transferred to your business.)

To register your business, you must have a written company constitution or choose to operate under the existing ASIC rules (called 'replaceable rules'). The constitution must cover issues such as:

¤ the powers of the directors

¤ the remuneration of the directors

- how directors will be appointed

- under what circumstances a meeting can be called

- how dividends will be paid (if any)

- how shares will be managed.

If you do not wish to draw up your own constitution, you can operate under ASIC's replaceable rules, which cover these issues. You can also choose to combine the replaceable rules with a constitution. Using just the replaceable rules can reduce costs when starting up, but make sure they are suitable for your business.

All companies must have directors and at least one member. You must have written confirmation from the people who are going to fill these roles. These written consents must be obtained before the application is made, but they are not submitted with the application; instead, they must be kept on file as part of the company's records.

Tax registrations

You will have to register for GST if:

- your business has an annual turnover of $50 000 or more

- you provide taxi travel as part of your business, regardless of your annual turnover.

You can register online at <www.business.gov.au>, or call the Tax Office and ask to have a form sent out to you. Registering for GST will entitle you to claim GST credits on any items you purchase, and you will also be required to charge your customers GST.

If you have an annual turnover of less than $50 000 (which you might in your early days), I still suggest registering for GST. It can cause accounting difficulties for other businesses that you deal with if you are not registered. I know of some companies that won't deal with anybody who is not GST registered. Not being registered also gives the impression that you are small, which you may be, but there's no need to advertise that. As the saying goes, 'Fake it till you make it'. If you are registered for GST you will be required to complete business activity statements (BAS). How often you are required to do this will depend on the size and circumstances of your business—most businesses complete a BAS each quarter.

If you are going to have employees, you will be required to register for pay as you go (PAYG) withholding. This enables you to withhold money from their pay and forward it to the Tax Office, along with your PAYG report as part of your activity statement. This is a component of each employee's taxation obligation. You must also register for PAYG withholding if you make a payment to a supplier who does not quote an ABN, because you must withhold part of this payment and forward it to the Tax Office.

Whatever your structure, you will also be required to obtain an ABN, which is a unique 11-digit number that identifies your business to the government, other businesses and your customers. Your ABN must be included on all of your business stationery, and all tax invoices and receipts. If you do not have an ABN, other businesses will be required to withhold tax from payments they make to you at a rate of 48.5 per cent. You may also require a new tax file number for your business, depending on the structure you have chosen. A tax file number identifies you or your business to the Tax Office.

You can apply for an ABN and a tax file number and register for GST and PAYG withholding all at the same time. You can apply online at the Australian Business Register site <abr.gov.au>, have the relevant forms sent to you from the Tax Office or ask your accountant to look after your application for you.

Registering a domain name

If you are going to set up a website, you will need to register a domain name. This is the unique address given to your website to enable people to find it. None of the registrations so far have any relation to registering a domain name—this is done separately.

There are many companies out there that can register your domain name (registering a domain name has nothing to do with the government). Shop around until you find the best price and service. (I recommend <www.godaddy.com>.) You can be do this online, and you will usually have to sign up for a year or two, after which time there will be a renewal fee. The domain name that you register must have some relevance to your business name, otherwise it will be rejected.

If you think the problem is bad now, just wait until we've solved it.
Arthur Kasspe

Other registrations

Depending on your business, there may be other registrations, permits or licences that you require. For example, if you are going to be offering financial advice, you must be licensed by ASIC to do so, and to operate as an electrician or plumber you will need a licence. Keep in mind that there may also be local government requirements. If you are going to work from home you may need a permit, depending on your business. Check out all levels of government—local, state and federal—to make sure your business is meeting all of its legal and registration requirements.

Pete's tip: make a list

Some of these registrations can be completed with one application, so before you start, make a list of the registrations you need, and do them in one go if you can.

$ $ $ $ $

Carefully consider what structure is most appropriate for your business and what registrations are required. Talk to a lawyer or an accountant and seek assistance from the relevant government department if needed. There are certain legal requirements to be met and your decisions will affect how you can run your business.

Chapter 10

From imagination to...

profitable publicity

> When we decided to launch an airline, Freddie Laker said that if I was
> going to take on American Airlines, United and British Airways, I would
> never have the advertising spend that they employ ... but if I went
> and made a bit of a fool of myself, I'd get on the front covers.
>
> **Richard Branson**

Key points

¤ You must know the difference between publicity and
   advertising.

¤ Publicity has the greatest potential to increase your sales at
   minimal cost.

¤ Publicity was the key to my success when selling the 'G.

Let me say up front that I can't emphasise enough how important
publicity can be to your business. If I had to choose a single
approach to generate lots of sales for minimal cost, it would be by
using publicity. Most of the success I had selling the 'G came from
the publicity I created. The press releases I wrote and sent out to
various media outlets attracted a huge amount of attention and
the more exposure I received the more frames I sold. Most of the
coverage I received was generated for virtually no cost. You can do
the same for your business.

Before we go any further, let's have a look at the difference between publicity and advertising.

Publicity versus advertising

Many people in business don't know the difference between advertising and publicity. The two have the same ultimate goal—to increase sales—but they are very different.

Advertising is when you pay for space or time to promote your product or service. You can do this in newspapers and magazines, on television, radio, billboards, on the side of a bus, in a cinema, on the side of a building—the possibilities are just about endless (and people are coming up with new ways and places to advertise all the time). You create your own advertising message, pay to have the ad created and then pay for the advertising space. Even a basic advertising campaign can cost thousands of dollars and some larger corporations spend millions of dollars on ad campaigns each year.

Publicity, on the other hand, is when you send out a media release, stage an event or do anything that attracts the media's attention. The aim is to have the media draw attention to your business for you. So, what's the biggest difference compared with advertising? Cost! Generating publicity can be done for next to nothing.

As an example, let's compare receiving the same amount of space in a newspaper through advertising and publicity. A reasonably large ad in a major daily newspaper could cost you thousands—or tens of thousands—of dollars. However, an article the same size about you or your business will only cost you the price of sending a fax. You don't have to pay for space or to have an ad designed. Just write a press release and surf the net to find out who to send it to and that's it. Think about that in terms of percentage return on dollars invested. It doesn't get much better for attracting attention and generating sales. And what about if you happened to get on television? You could end up as one of those feelgood stories at the end of the news or maybe you will be featured on *Today Tonight* because of the revolutionary new product you have invented. How much would that air time have cost you in the form of advertising? More than most small businesses can afford.

Publicity can give you massive exposure for just a few dollars—it generates sales and it creates awareness about your product or service. Publicity is the cheapest form of marketing that exists and it produces the biggest gains. Used properly, publicity can make you rich.

The halo effect

There is another major benefit of using publicity. It's extremely difficult to build a good reputation through advertising, but publicity can instantly give you and your business a positive image. This is referred to as the 'halo effect'.

When any business or person places an advert in the newspaper (or any media), they are automatically seen simply as an advertiser—just another person with a sales pitch designed to sell you something you don't really need. People can be turned off by ads. You have to not only persuade readers that they can benefit from your offer, you also have to convince them that you do have their best interests at heart, that you are honest, that your prices are fair, that your product is safe ... you get the idea.

But when the media runs a story about you or your business, you don't have this problem. You are no longer a salesperson or a money-hungry businessperson. When people see you in the news portrayed in a positive way, they will assume that you are reputable and honest—you are someone to be trusted. The public assumes that the media has done its research and has thoroughly checked out your credentials and the quality of your product or service. It's almost as if the media has given you its stamp of approval.

> **Pete's tip: go your own way**
>
> *If you do what everybody else does, you'll never be able to set your business apart. Many businesses focus on advertising simply because they think that it's the only way to attract attention to their business. Be different—use publicity to build your business.*

Being featured in the media also gives the perception that you are an expert in your field. People naturally assume that you would only be interviewed on a particular topic if you are an expert on that subject. Nobody would interview me about my cooking skills, but I've done many interviews about sports memorabilia.

> When somebody writes an article about you and it is published in a newspaper or a magazine, or when you appear as a guest on a radio or TV show, you gain credibility and celebrity.
> **Dan Kennedy — *No B.S. Sales Success***

Let's have a look at Richard Branson as a perfect example of somebody who understands the benefits of publicity and has benefited from the halo effect. Branson has a reputation as a fun-loving guy. He comes across in the media as being friendly and outgoing, with a wide smile and shaggy hair. He certainly seems trustworthy. Branson wants people to see his businesses in the same way and he has succeeded at this because of publicity. It would have been impossible for Branson to generate the same image for his company through advertising alone. Portraying himself in his own ads as friendly and outgoing won't work—of course he would present himself like that! But when the media presents him this way, it comes across as genuine, because the media outlets are controlling what you see and hear, not Branson or Virgin. This is the halo effect and it can benefit you and your business.

Pete's tip: the halo effect

Publicity can give you and your business credibility and a positive image that is impossible to achieve using advertising alone.

Many companies waste millions of dollars trying to establish an image or brand using advertising. When it comes to branding, too much money can sometimes be worse than too little—if you have a lot of money you may be tempted to spend it on stupid things like AFL grand final commercials. Brands are built on what other people are saying about you, not what you're saying about yourself.

Some of the advantages of using publicity are:

- ¤ It costs a fraction of the cost of advertising.

- ¤ It's fun.

- ¤ It produces the 'halo effect', something that advertising can never do.

- ¤ It's fun.

- ¤ It generates sales.

- ¤ It increases profits.

- ¤ It gives you a positive image.

- ¤ Oh yeah, and it's fun!

Just think about how jealous all the companies that paid tens of thousands of dollars to be featured on radio and television, and in newspapers and magazines, will be when they find out you received the same coverage for *free* (well, practically; it only costs 50¢ to print your press release and fax it). You are already one step ahead of your competitors who have to cover the cost of advertising. With no advertising costs, you can start making profits right away.

This is not to say that you shouldn't use advertising at all. A well-designed ad campaign could be great for your business (advertising is the subject of the next chapter). But be aware of the differences between advertising and publicity and the benefits of each. A combination of the two is good for most businesses, though you should rely more on publicity when you are getting started because you will most likely have limited funds. I also believe that—for the reasons given above—publicity will bring more benefits to your company than advertising.

> You can buy a person's hands but you can't buy his heart.
> His heart is where his enthusiasm, his loyalty is.
> **Stephen Covey**

The press release

Of course, it's not *quite* as simple as sending out a press release and then waiting for the onslaught to begin. You must come up with an angle that will attract the media's attention. 'New soft drink with 20 per cent more bubbles' won't do it, nor will '24-hour convenience store opens'. How about '21 year old sells MCG for under $500'? Now that's more like it!

The aim of a press release

The aim of a press release is not as obvious as you might think. Most people will tell you the aim of a press release is to attract attention to your business and to increase your sales. This is incorrect. These are the overall aims of your publicity campaign, but the press release itself has only one single goal: *to get you an interview*.

The press release is designed to draw in members of the media so that they will contact you for more information. Your press release is not meant to be printed word for word in the media (as often happens). If it is, you have written an appealing and pleasing press release but, unfortunately, not a successful one. If you send out your press release and it is printed word for word in the local press, that is the only coverage you are going to receive—that's because you've already told the reporters everything they need to know. Why would members of the press bother wasting their own time and resources calling you for an interview when all of their questions have already been answered? Structure your release so that the media will be enticed to give you a call.

> **Pete's tip: building a brand**
>
> *Brands are built on what other people are saying about you, not what you're saying about yourself.*

Writing a press release

You will get that call for an interview if you have a good 'hook' in your press release so that the journalist can see a 'story' in it. Once again, we're going fishing! A hook is something that will prompt journalists to give you a call because they want to know more. For me, the best hook was '21 year old sells MCG for under $500'. This attracts interest on a number of levels:

- I'm young—always a good angle for a news story.

- I'm selling the MCG—how do you do that?

- I'm selling it for under $500—how do you do *that*?

This is a simple hook that attracts attention as soon as the press release arrives. Think about your product or business and about your USP. What headline could you put on your release that will have a journalist instantly reaching for the phone to find out more? You may have something that people have never seen before. Maybe you are a bit controversial or contentious, or perhaps you can solve a problem for people. You can also use current events as a hook. Perhaps you can find a football angle at grand final time, an Easter angle at Easter or a beach angle at the start of summer.

Once you have a headline you must put enough information in the release to entice the journalist, but not too much or they won't need to contact you. Keep it to *one page*. If your release is longer than this, you are giving too much detail.

The main body of a press release is broken into four segments:

- introductory summary

- quotations

- credentials

- call to action.

Although it is a requirement for all good press releases to have these four segments, the press release need not be limited to four paragraphs—as long as it fits on one A4 page. Let's have a look at each of these four points, using some examples from my selling the 'G press releases.

The introductory summary, as the name suggests, must always come first, and it must contain in a few sentences all the important information you are trying to convey. It's the who, what, why, where and when. For example, one of my MCG releases began as follows:

> A 21-year-old sports fanatic and AFL member is now selling the MCG to the widespread public — in pieces. He is giving the public a chance to own a part of Australian Sporting History which is set to disappear after this year's AFL Grand Final when the rest of the MCC Pavilion is set to be demolished.
>
> Peter Williams is giving sporting fanatics and the widespread public the opportunity to obtain framed sections of the MCC Crested Carpet that once lay in the Ponsford Stand.

This sums up the venture.

The second segment of the press release is the quotation section. This is where you back up what you've already stated in your introductory summary. The quotation is a supporting statement provided by you. The only time it is okay to quote someone else is if it is a testimonial about you or your business.

One of my press release quotes was:

> 'People are so passionate about Aussie Rules, cricket and the MCG,' states Williams. 'I don't want to see a big part of our culture simply die. I want to give everyone the chance to have a piece of Australian history and sporting legacy hanging in their homes, bars and offices.'

The next step is to include your credentials. Why should people listen to you about this topic? This is easy. Simply state why you are an expert. Maybe it's your years of experience or your qualifications or you have written a book on the subject. Perhaps it's all three!

The final section is a call to action. This is also self-explanatory. Tell the journalist what to do next. For example, one call to action I used was: 'For further media enquires please contact Peter Williams direct on XXXX XXXX'. Make sure you provide contact details and a specific contact name. Don't just use your business name and don't just provide your phone number. Always include something such as:

¤ 'To schedule an interview, contact ...'

¤ 'For more information on ... contact ...'

¤ 'Interviews can be arranged by contacting ... directly on ...'

Remember, the aim of your press release is to secure an interview, so make it easy for journalists to arrange this, and show that you are wanting, willing and able.

Sending it out

To send out my releases, I simply looked up contact details on the internet, and then faxed and emailed local and major newspapers, magazines, and television and radio stations. This is the cheap and easy way to do it. I later used the services of AAP MediaNet <www.aapmedianet.com.au>, who flooded the media with the release. It does cost money to use this type of service, but it can make the job a lot easier (leverage your time!) and it will ensure your release is sent out across a wide range of mediums. It is also a professional way to get in touch with media outlets. You can also use this service to send your release to a specific target audience, which might help to increase your response rate.

Download:
For a comprehensive home study course on how to make bucketloads of cash from free publicity — including examples, step-by-step instructions on what to include, and instructions for layout, writing a headline and looking professional — visit the online store at <www.preneurmarketing.com.au> and check out 'Unleashing the Power of Publicty'. During the checkout process enter the code 'UPPDISC' to receive a 30 per cent discount.

Selling the 'G with publicity

Here are some of the press releases I used to sell the 'G. They are all written according to the method outlined above and they all worked — extremely well!

Workbook:

Complete your first press release in your From Imagination to Implementation Workbook.

Read through them to get an idea of how to put a press release together, and what to include and what to leave out. Note the slightly different angles, especially for the release sent to the Geelong newspapers. You can do this too. If you have an attachment to, for example, a certain location or organisation, write a press release specifically for this. Take advantage of anything that will attract the media to you and your business but don't forget publicity will also help the association and organisations you are involved with.

       FOR FURTHER INFORMATION CALL:
PETER WILLIAMS — XXXX XXXX

21 YEAR OLD SELLS MCG—
FOR UNDER $500

A 21-year-old sports fanatic and AFL member is now selling the MCG to the widespread public — in pieces. He is giving the public a chance to own a part of Australian Sporting History which is set to disappear after this year's AFL Grand Final when the rest of the MCC Pavilion is set to be demolished.

Peter Williams is giving sporting fanatics and the widespread public the opportunity to obtain framed sections of the MCC Crested Carpet that once lay in the Ponsford Stand.

'People are so passionate about Aussie Rules, cricket and the MCG', states Williams. 'I don't want to see a big part of our culture simply die. I want to give everyone the chance to have a piece of Australian history and sporting legacy hanging in their homes, bars and offices.'

'This is a exceptional and unprecedented opportunity', Sports Memorabilia Specialist David Fenech of Frame-Mem Collectables said. 'Collectors are frantic when it comes to celebrities' autographs, this is one better. Athletes and celebrities can sign infinitely, whereas this specific carpet is limited and can never be reproduced ... an opportunity too good to pass up.'

In addition to the limited MCC Crested Carpet, Williams is offering a small quantity of the pieces framed in authentic timber that also was once located in the now demolished Ponsford Stand, which saw over 30 years of sporting excellence.

Those wanting to purchase their own certified authentic piece of the MCG should visit <www.SportingLimitedEditions.com>.

Further media enquires to Peter Williams on XXXX XXXX or pjwilli@XXXXXXXX.net.au

###

FOR IMMEDIATE RELEASE

FOR FURTHER INFORMATION CALL:
PETER WILLIAMS — XXXX XXXX

MCG GOING BUT WILL NOT BE FORGOTTEN

Thanks to the entrepreneurial efforts of a young 21 year old, the MCG and its world famous MCC pavilion will not go unforgotten in the near future. E.J. Whitten Foundation supporter Peter Williams is endeavouring to save Australia's sporting history by giving sports fans and Australians at large the chance to own part of the MCG and Australian History — well a piece anyway.

Williams is keeping the spirit of the ground alive throughout homes, bars and offices Australia-wide by selling pieces of the now demolished Ponsford stand. He is giving fans and collectors the opportunity to obtain framed pieces of MCC Crested carpet, which once lay in the now demolished stand, while donating 10 per cent of each sale to Mr Football — the E.J. Whitten Foundation.

'We are trying to celebrate the MCG's 150th birthday and give what the MCG calls the 'People's Ground' back to the people', Williams said whilst on hand and knee cleaning and preserving the famous carpet. 'This is a part of Aussie culture and once the rest of the development goes ahead (after the 2003 AFL Grand Final), a part of our spirit is set to die. I'm just trying to see that it doesn't completely get forgotten about, it's too important.'

Peter is packing this piece of history in triple-matted frames, put together by expert sporting memorabilia framer, Dave Fenech of Sports Mem Collectables, with a series of photos of the MCG in its glory days, AFL and Test Match Cricket, along with a plaque outlining its history and limited status. Peter was also lucky enough to save some timber from the stand as well, and is using the authentic timber as framing for a limited number of these pieces.

People wishing to help keep Australian history alive and support the E.J. Whitten Foundation can view and obtain a piece of the MCG at a website Pete has developed and designed himself, <www.SportingLimitedEditions.com>.

For media enquires and to help with the campaign to 'Save the MCG and MCC Memory' call Pete direct on XXXX XXXX.

###

FOR IMMEDIATE RELEASE
FOR FURTHER INFORMATION CALL:
PETER WILLIAMS — XXXX XXXX

LOCAL DEAKIN GRADUATE SELLS MCG—FOR LESS THAN $500

A Commerce graduate from Geelong's own Deakin University is currently selling the MCG to the widespread public — in pieces. He is giving the public a chance to own a part of Australian Sporting History which is set to disappear after this year's AFL Grand Final when the rest of the MCC Pavilion is set to be demolished.

21-year-old Peter Williams is using the knowledge from the marketing and management majors, which were part of his Deakin degree, and giving sporting fanatics and the widespread public the opportunity to obtain framed sections of the MCC Crested Carpet that once lay in the Ponsford Stand.

'People are so passionate about Aussie Rules, cricket and the MCG', states Williams. 'I don't want to see a big part of our culture simply die. I want to give everyone the chance to have a piece of Australian history and sporting legacy hanging in their homes, bars and offices. The base Deakin Geelong gave me has given me the knowledge and confidence to make this happen.'

'This is an exceptional and unprecedented opportunity', Sports Memorabilia Specialist David Fenech of Frame-Mem Collectables said. 'Collectors are frantic when it comes to celebrities' autographs, this is one better. Athletes and celebrities can sign infinitely, whereas this specific carpet is limited and can never be reproduced . . . an opportunity to' good to pass up.'

In addition to the limited MCC Crested Carpet, Williams is offering a small quantity of the pieces framed in authentic timber that also was once located in the now demolished Ponsford Stand, which saw over 30 years of sporting excellence.

Those wanting to purchase their own certified authentic piece of the MCG should visit <www.SportingLimitedEditions.com>.

Further media enquiries to Peter Williams on XXXX XXXX or pjwilli@XXXXXXXX.net.au

###

FOR IMMEDIATE RELEASE   **FOR FURTHER INFORMATION CALL:**
PETER WILLIAMS — XXXX XXXX

OWN A PIECE OF THE MCG ALL FOR THE COST OF A PIE, CHIPS & A DRINK!

Sports Fanatic and young entrepreneur Peter Williams is giving Australians the opportunity to own part of Australia's number 1 historic sporting ground for less than a pie, chips and beer at the footy.

During the recent re-development of the Ponsford Stand much of the prized and time-honoured timber was left lying around. That was before 21-year-old Williams saw an opportunity and acted quickly to save it!

'I'm trying to celebrate the MCG's 150th birthday and give what the MCG calls the 'People's Ground' back to the people', Williams said. 'This is a part of Aussie culture and once the rest of the development goes ahead (after the 2003 AFL Grand Final), a part of our sporting heritage is set to die. I'm just trying to see that it doesn't completely get forgotten, it's too important.'

The public can purchase a limited number of authentic 5"× 7" certificates outlining the story and history of the world famous ground and attached to the document is an authenticated piece of the unique timber from the Ponsford Stand.

Best of all, Williams is giving the public the unique opportunity to own part of Australian history, for merely the cost of covering the administration plus postage and handling.

'When it's all said and done', Williams said, 'This is a chance for all Australians to own a piece of MCG magic for less than a beer, pie and chips at the footy!'

Certificates make ideal gifts, either as collectables or to commemorate the great times shared at and in the MCG.

All that is required to obtain a piece of sporting culture is either to mail a cheque or mail order, to cover the postage and packaging of $9.90, to P.O. Box XXXX, Geelong, Victoria 3220, call XXXX XXXX or visit <www.SportingLimitedEditions.com>.

For further media enquires please contact Peter Williams direct on XXXX XXXX.

###

Following are examples of the press I received as a result of sending out the releases. I was contacted for each of these articles and the papers also sent out a photographer to take a picture of me with the frames and the carpet. So you can see that the press releases were a success. They caught the attention of the journalists from the beginning (the first step), but then, more importantly, I was contacted for further information and this resulted in a story, rather than just a word-for-word reproduction of my press release.

Publicity can also have a domino effect, which is what happened in my case. All media outlets keep an eye on each other and follow up on any stories that they think they could use as well. Once my story started to circulate, I received media enquiries from outlets that the releases hadn't even been sent to.

You also never know what might happen once your press release starts circulating. I had given a copy of one of my releases to my friend Steve McKnight <www.propertyinvesting.com>, who was in the middle of a publicity whirlwind of his own due to the huge success of his book *From 0 to 130 Properties in 3.5 Years*. Steve was working with *Today Tonight* on a series of stories about his Millionaire Apprentice Program (in which I was a participant, and which became the focus of his second book) and happened to pass my release on to one of the *Today Tonight* journalists. Next thing you know I receive a call from Channel 7 News for an interview.

These examples are just to give you an idea of the type of coverage you can receive. There were many more articles and I also made several television and radio appearances. The majority of my sales were made as a result of this publicity.

Figure 10.1: 'Magical Carpet Ride'

Magical carpet ride

CHRIS TINKLER

A BUDGING Richard Branson could be on a roll — with MCG carpet.

Pete Williams, 21, has snatched up the rare MCG carpet and old Ponsford Stand timber from a wrecker for a nominal fee and packaged them as a prized piece of sporting history.

The Victorian entrepreneur is selling 900 authenticated squares of the MCC-crested carpet that once lay in the dining room of the Ponsford Stand, which was demolished for the MCG redevelopment.

A hundred of the squares, framed in timber from the famous stand, are on sale for

$588, including GST and postage. The remaining 800, in standard frames, are going for $452.

A commerce graduate, AFL member, sports memorabilia collector and Essendon fan, Mr Williams said he was inspired by the story of New Jersey man Paul Hartunian, who sold pieces of the Brooklyn Bridge in the 1980s.

"With the redevelopment of the MCG, I thought there could be a similar opportunity," he said.

"Also, I didn't want to see a big part of our

culture simply die. People are so passionate about Aussie rules, cricket and the MCG.

"I want to give everyone the chance to have a piece of Australian history and sporting legacy hanging in their homes, bars or offices."

Mr Williams, of Bacchus Marsh, is donating 10 per cent of the proceeds of each sale to the EJ Whitten Foundation, which assists prostate cancer research.

The carpet pieces went on sale two weeks ago, with about 25 sold so far.

To purchase a piece, visit www.sporting limitededitions.com or phone 0417 071 111.

Passionate: Pete Williams with his unique pieces of MCG history. Picture: FAITH NULLEY

Sunday Herald Sun, 3 August 2003, p. 25.

Source: The Herald & Weekly Times/The Herald & Weekly Times Photographic Collection

'EJ's lap preserved in print'

Herald Sun, 10 June 2004

'In the lead-up to the E.J. Whitten Legends Game at Telstra Dome on June 25, which will raise funds for prostate cancer research via the E.J. Whitten Foundation, 1000 framed photographs are available of "Mr Football" and his son Ted Jnr taken during their lap of honour.'

'Peter carpeted and scores well'

By Chris Riches, *Express Telegraph,* 5 August 2003

'Thanks to enterprising young local Peter Williams, the distinctive MCC crested carpet was rescued from the rubbish heap brought about by the demolition of the MCG's Ponsford Stand and is now for sale — in small sections of course — to keen momorabilia hunters.'

'Buy a piece of the 'G' cheap as chips'

Collectormania, no. 98, December 2003

'Sports fanatic and young entrepreneur Peter Williams is giving Australians the opportunity to own part of Australia's No. 1 historic sporting ground for less than the cost of a pie, chips and a beer at the footy.'

Chapter 11

From imagination to...

effective marketing

> You should be dedicating 50 per cent of your time to running your
> business and the other 50 per cent to marketing your business.
>
> **Brad Sugars — marketing expert and author**

Key points

¤ Use the Preneur Marketing Hierarchy to get the right message
  to the right people.

¤ Start at the bottom of the hierarchy and work your way up.

¤ Use the AIDA principle (attention, interest, desire, action) to
  create successful ads.

The key to effective marketing is not large headlines, bright colours
or an eye-catching image. Sure, these things will help attract
attention to your ad, but the aim of a marketing campaign is not
simply to have people notice the ad. The aim is for them to notice
the ad and then purchase from you. The first step means nothing
without the second. The key to successful marketing is reaching
the *right people* with the *right message* using the *right advertising* at
the *right time* for your business.

It is with this in mind that I developed the Preneur Marketing Hierarchy, a system that allows you to tailor your advertising to different groups of people — from those who are existing customers through to those who have never heard of you or your product — in a manner that grows your business. This is something that many businesses give little thought to. For many organisations an advertising campaign often simply means buying some newspaper space, putting up a billboard and recording a few radio ads. There may be some talk about demographics and putting the ads in the right place but this is not nearly enough to ensure your ads result in profits. It also means spending money on ads that are not sufficiently targeted, resulting in wasted money. Before you start thinking about whether you should use fluoro orange or bright red in your ad, think about who it will be easiest for you to sell to, where these people are in relation to your product (from regular customer to 'never heard of you') and how you can reach them. Correctly targeting your advertising will give you a better result for a lower cost.

As you will see, the Preneur Marketing Hierarchy gives you a framework to support and structure your marketing. This structure is aligned with the growth of a new business (or any business):

¤ From a *resistance* perspective, you will see that the 'prospects' at the base of the hierarchy are more receptive to purchasing from you, with resistance growing as you move up. Obviously a good place to start!

¤ From a *cash flow* perspective, moving up the hierarchy and successfully 'conquering' a lower level will provide cash flow for the upper levels.

¤ From a *cost* perspective, as you move up the hierarchy the costs of marketing your business to the next level of suspects increases, so it is smart to start at the base.

When you can identify these trends and factors you will find that the process of marketing your business becomes systematic, rather than ad hoc.

The Preneur Marketing Hierarchy

The Preneur Marketing Hierarchy shows you how to focus your marketing. This is especially useful in the early days of your business, where funds are usually tight and a poorly planned ad can be a very costly mistake.

Once you have identified your market, be smart about your marketing. The hierarchy exists within the target demographic that you have located, however, not everyone is going to buy from you—there will be different levels of intrigue within your audience. Some will not be interested, while some people will be but will have to overcome inertia. The smart thing to do with your marketing budget is to sell to the most likely prospects first. This is what the Preneur Marketing Hierarchy is all about—giving you a hierarchy or structure to follow to maximise your marketing dollars. It is based on the premise that past and existing customers are the easiest people to sell to, while people who have never heard of you are the most difficult. And there are a number of different levels in between. Pretty obvious stuff, right? I believe that this is the most important aspect of your marketing. Many businesses can put together an eye-catching, attention-grabbing ad, but using the Preneur Marketing Hierarchy will put you ahead of the pack in terms of effectiveness and costs.

Let's compare two groups at the opposite ends of the marketing scale. At the bottom of the hierarchy are people who have purchased from you before and were happy with the experience. At the other end of the scale (the top of the hierarchy), we have the people who have no idea that your product exists, no knowledge of your company and would not even know where to start looking for you if they did have an inkling that you existed.

Now, which of these groups would you rather try to sell to? Of course, that's an easy question to answer. Yet many businesses—without even realising—head straight to the top of the hierarchy, where it's much more difficult and much more expensive. They take out large newspaper ads, put up billboards near busy roads and even put an ad on television (if the budget stretches that far). This is done with the belief that it's good to reach as many people as possible because then you have a greater chance of getting your message across to potential customers. But without proper consideration of the marketing hierarchy, this is like sitting in the middle of the Pacific Ocean with a fishing rod. Sure there are more fish around, but they're not going to come near you in the middle of the sea. The smart thing to do is find the small ponds—there may not be as many fish, but you'll actually be able to catch some of these! Only when you have successfully fished the smaller ponds do you head out to sea.

The five levels of the Preneur Marketing Hierarchy are shown in the figure 11.1.

Figure 11.1: the Preneur Marketing Hierarchy

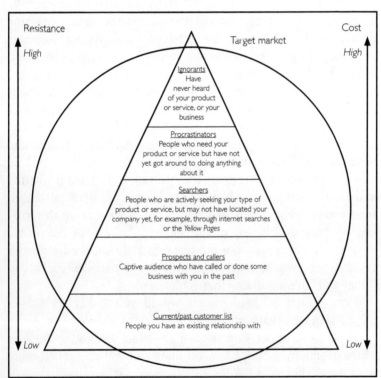

The easiest prospects to sell to are at the bottom (least resistance) and the hardest are at the top (most resistance). You should start at the bottom and for each level you should have a different message and use different techniques to reach it. For example, you don't need to post large billboards to reach your regular customers, but you may need to advertise on television to reach people who have never heard of you, your product or your service. Also, if you are trying to reach any of the levels with, for example, print advertising, the message (hook, header, tag lines) will need to be different for each level, even when using the same medium.

> **Pete's tip: start at the bottom**
>
> *You will encounter the least resistance at the bottom of the hierarchy, so start there. Don't move on to the next level until you have adequate systems in place to cater for the current level.*

Let's have a look at the different levels of the hierarchy, addressing how you can reach each group and what the message should be. We'll start at the bottom.

Current/past customer list

The people at the bottom of the hierarchy are people who are currently your customers, or who have been in the past. It doesn't matter how, or why, they initially came to you—they are yours now, so the aim is to keep them.

Assuming that they have had good experiences with your business, this will be the easiest group to sell to because:

¤ You don't have to educate them from scratch about your product or your business. If they have purchased from you before, they have most likely already browsed through your range, know what you offer and what it costs, and are familiar with your payment methods and terms. Also, they have probably already compared you with the competition and decided in your favour.

¤ Their previous good experience will encourage them to purchase from you again. We've all had the experience of finding a business that provides really good service, so we go back to it in the future.

¤ You should already have collected their details, so they will be easy to contact. There are a number of ways to do this. You can simply have a mailing list sign-up form on your website or in your store, or you can start a 'club' where members receive a discount, say 5 per cent. You could even run a competition and collect details that way. A common technique is to have people drop their business cards in a box to enter a competition. (However you collect details, make sure that people know they are going on a mailing list. Under privacy laws it is illegal to misuse information collected from your customers, and sending people marketing material when they weren't aware that they had signed up is a guaranteed way to infuriate people and lose business.)

The wise marketer realizes that marketing doesn't end
with the sale ... it just takes a new direction.
The Entrepreneur Network

Reaching the current/past customer list

One of the best and most cost-effective ways to reach current or past customers is through direct mail using your mailing list, either via snail mail or email. Write a sales letter that will entice your customers. (There are many businesses out there that can help you write good sales letters—use leverage!) Remember the hierarchy, though—these people have already signed up to your mailing list, so you know they are interested. There's no need for hard selling here, just inform them of your latest products and perhaps a special offer you have running at the moment. Include a brochure of your latest range of products or services and maybe even a voucher to encourage them to visit your store or website. Treat these people as friends and address them in this manner.

You can also send out a fortnightly or monthly newsletter (weekly is too often). Your newsletter should include useful information, so that people will read it, and also some advertising material to alert readers to your latest offers. So, if you run a nursery, your last newsletter before summer may include an article about what flowers should be planted at this time of year. Next to this article, you may have an ad that reads '10 per cent off all summer plants'. You are providing your customers with an added service (the article) and reaching them with your advertising at the same time. If the newsletter contains useful articles, you will gain regular readers. If possible, address your direct mail and newsletters personally to recipients.

Other ways to reach this group are:

¤ Start a club for your customers where they receive exclusive discounts.

¤ Send out a follow-up letter after they have made a purchase. This reminds them about your business and also shows that their custom is appreciated.

¤ Offer a bonus service — for example, buy a mountain bike and receive a free service in six months' time. This encourages the customer to return to the store.

You can also ask existing customers for referrals. Give them 5 per cent off if they come back with a friend or give them free movie tickets if they sign somebody up to your newsletter. If you have provided an out-of-this-world experience, people will be happy to recommend you.

Your message for the current/past customer list

As I've said, these are people who have already purchased from you, so there is no need to beat them over the head with your ads. You don't need to explain explicitly why they need your industry's product or service (as you have to do with those at the top of the hierarchy, who are oblivious). When I say 'industry's product or service', I am referring to the generic items you sell — such as cars, paint or computers—not the specifics of your unique offering (which you have defined in your USP, right?). Instead focus your message on your new products and current promotions. You can also include a special offer exclusively for past customers, which can be redeemed by presenting the follow-up letter you sent them. This will make them feel valued and keep them coming back. For example, the company I buy my software from has a 'smart buy' program, where you collect certificates each time you buy and can redeem these for a discount on a later purchase. Combine this with the already low prices and great service, and I no longer shop around for my software—I just go straight to this store. Other great examples aimed at retaining existing customers are airline frequent-flyer programs and store discount cards.

Costs in reaching your current/past customer list

When starting your business, you will most likely have limited cash (actually, even if you have bucketloads of cash you should still start here—why spend money when you don't have to?). It's more effective to communicate with and market to people you already have a relationship with. You can start at the cheap end of the spectrum, with mail-outs and an email newsletter, and you can also market to customers when they purchase from you, which costs you nothing. There is no need for expensive newspaper ads, *Yellow Pages* ads or a television campaign. Simply putting a coupon in with the product is effective and virtually free.

It's important that you have these systems and processes in place as everyone you sell to at any point, now or in the future, will fall into this category. So spend some time early on to design your 'current/past customer' systems.

Prospects and callers

This level of the hierarchy contains people who have contacted your business—either by calling, visiting your website or wandering into your store—but have not yet made a purchase. These people are in your sales pipeline as they are in contact with you. They know enough about you to have contacted you, and they are ready to buy, but you have not yet made a sale. People will be 'moved' into your prospects level from higher levels once they respond to your marketing. *Sales and Marketing* magazine states that most businesses spend 94 per cent of their marketing budget on getting the phone to ring (through various advertising) but only 6 per cent on marketing to the prospect when he or she calls. By getting your systems in place for this level, a level all your customers go through, you will be ahead of the game.

As you can see, the Preneur Marketing Hierarchy is dynamic and your target market is not static—so don't treat it like it is.

Reaching the prospects and callers

You must put systems in place to maximise your interaction with prospects such as follow-up campaigns and professional sales techniques. For example, The Athlete's Foot chain has what it calls the '*greet* and *seat*' rules, which is a seven-step process that aims to provide prospects with help in making their purchasing decision. It's a system The Athlete's Foot put in place, like you must, to 'milk' every dollar it can from its advertising. Getting a person through the door is just the first step—it does not secure a sale.

Here are some techniques you can use to communicate with people who have contacted you:

- Have a package prepared to send out to people who contact you, even those who just make an inquiry. Don't ask if they would like a package, instead assume that they will, 'Let me send you some more information about us. Can I have your address please?'

- Have an on-hold advertising message on your phone system. Research has found that 70 per cent of callers are put on hold and the average hold time is 43 seconds. If that is 43 seconds of silence or elevator music, what a wasted opportunity! You have these prospects on hold for hundreds of hours every year. It's the most captive audience you'll ever have to market to.

- If it is appropriate for your business, ask your customers if they would like to make an appointment, or offer to go to see them at no charge.

¤ Have advertising in your store or on your website about your current special offers to reach people who are just browsing.

¤ If you have a newsletter, place a sign-up field in a prominent position on your website, to encourage people who are just browsing to sign up. Don't make people fill out a complicated form, because many won't bother. There's really only one important detail — their email address. You can conduct further research later if you require more information.

¤ Professional quoting is essential. If you are looking at starting a 'trade' business — such as being a concreter or a plumber — whatever you do, put a system in place to make your quotes professional. A quote is nothing more than a tradie's name for a proposal. So when you quote on a job, don't just write it on a carbon-backed note pad. Put a system in place to include a letter, a sheet of testimonials and the quote.

Most businesses differentiate themselves from their competitors in their advertising but forget about differentiating when they are face to face with a prospect. Creating appropriate systems to deal with prospects will blow your competition out of the water.

Your message for prospects and callers

These people have done enough research to make contact, so again there should be no need to overtly educate them about your industry's product or service — they know they need the product or service or they would not have walked through the door or picked up the phone. You are instead trying to encourage them to make that first purchase from *your* business rather than your competition. Here are some suggestions:

¤ Espouse the benefits of your product or service in your messages (think about your USP).

¤ Advertise a discount for new customers in your message (for example, internet service providers often have a discounted rate for new customers for the first six months).

- Use testimonials to support your claims of superiority.

- Promote your latest products or services.

- Use the AIDA principles discussed later in this chapter.

- Ask questions to show you care.

Costs for reaching the prospects and callers

As these people have responded to other advertising, you are now communicating to people who are receptive to you and are predisposed to buy, so the costs are lower as there is no inertia to overcome. With many of these systems there are only up-front costs in time and money (such as sales-system development and on-hold messaging). Yes there will be costs in printing the proposals (quotes), but you will be able to judge through the one-on-one interactions with prospects if they are 'hot or not' and what will close the sale.

Pete's tip: don't refer people to the *Yellow Pages*

It always amazes me when people say 'You'll find us in the Yellow Pages'. *This may be true, but you will also find the competition! Don't give people the chance to be enticed by your competitors. Include your direct contact details in your advertising, and never refer people to the phone book.*

Promise, large promise, is the soul of an advertisement.
Samuel Johnson — author

Searchers (often called tyre-kickers)

The searchers are just at the beginning of the buying cycle. They have decided they need a particular product or service and so have started looking for it, most often through an internet search or in directories. They are trying to find the best item and company to buy from. These people are currently looking for your product or service to fix a problem they have, so ask yourself where will these prospects look? These people *have not yet contacted your business* in any way, so we are now looking at how you will advertise—for example, in the directories or through search engines—in order to encourage them to contact you.

You will notice that we are now at the third level of the hierarchy and the cost of advertising is starting to increase in line with the level of resistance. Also, keep in mind that in the *Yellow Pages* and on search engines, your ad appears right next to the ads of your competitors, so you must make an effort to make your ad stand out.

Reaching the searchers

Searchers are best reached through advertising in directories (such as the *Yellow Pages*) and on search engines, because these people know they need your industry's product and are doing their initial research for a supplier. They are not yet a 'prospect' as they have not contacted you—they are doing their preliminary research on providers to see who they are willing to become prospects for. Keep in mind that people are usually ready to buy at this stage.

Here are some suggestions for making the most of your *Yellow Pages* advertising:

¤ Research has shown that people call businesses with the larger ads first. A larger ad usually provides a disproportionate increase in responses—for example, an ad that is 50 per cent larger may only cost 25 per cent more but generate a 200 per cent increase in calls.

¤ Tell these people how you are going to solve their problem. Do you have the lowest prices? The quickest delivery? The longest opening hours? Include the benefits of your product or service and your USP. Remember, your ad will be sitting right next to those of your competitors.

¤ Use colour in your ad if you can afford it and place a heavy border around it. These embellishments will make your ad stand out.

¤ Include as much useful information in your ad as you can.

- Include your logo, as this will help build company or brand recognition.

- Use the AIDA principles discussed later in this chapter to create an attention-grabbing ad.

Research has shown that people look at an average of five ads when browsing the *Yellow Pages*, so make sure you get their attention.

When you set up a website, don't assume that your business will show up in search engines, especially when you get started. Your business may be buried on page 27 of a search, meaning most people won't find you. An alternative is to run a search-engine advertising campaign—for example, using Google Adwords or Yahoo! Search Marketing. This will ensure that your ad appears more prominently when a search is performed. Using the internet is discussed in detail in chapter 13.

Your message for the searchers

Remember that the searchers have not actually contacted your business yet, so you must encourage them to visit your website or give you a call. They are searching because they are ready to buy and have a problem that needs solving, so make your ad reflect how you will help them. If you are in the business of repairing computers, make your headline something like: 'Computer repairs: we'll be at your door in one hour'. Ensure your contact details are prominent and conclude your ad with a call to action: 'Call us now to see how we can help' or 'Our friendly staff are waiting to help you'.

As with the prospects and callers, advertising to this group could:

- espouse the benefits of your product or service

- advertise a discount for new customers

- promote your current sales or discounts.

A *Yellow Pages* ad will appear for a year, so instead of using your current sales, you might simply advertise, say, $50 cash back for first-time customers.

You do not need to overtly sell these people your industry's product or your service, because they are already looking for it. Instead, you must sell them on your business. For example, if you google 'on hold advertising' and click on our ad, you go straight to a landing page created purely for Google click-thrus. Why? Because people who have searched for 'on hold advertising' don't need to be sold on the idea. They already want it. They're trying to choose a company to buy from, so I send them straight to a customised page to encourage them to sign up with my company. (This page is the 'landing page' for my Google campaign.) The general home page, on the other hand, includes information about why on-hold advertising is so useful and then as people go deeper into the site they learn about the benefits of the company. It's all about understanding what information the different groups are after and making it as easy as possible for them to find it.

Download:

For a free Yellow Pages advertising report (by Shannon Curtis), go to <www.preneurmarketing. com.au/yellowpages.php>.

Procrastinators

Procrastinators are those who know they need your product or service, but just haven't done anything about it. Finding your product or service to fix their 'problem' is not high on their to-do list or causing them enough pain to make them take action. As the resistance level increases your advertising can start to become more expensive.

Reaching the procrastinators

Procrastinators are not actively searching the internet to find you, they are not going to look for you in the phone book and they are not just going to wander into your store. So how do you reach them?

Here are some suggestions:

¤ Advertise in local or daily newspapers, or magazines. Procrastinators may not be searching for you but they can still be attracted by an ad in the newspaper. Use the AIDA principles discussed later in this chapter.

¤ Conduct a mail-out. You won't have contact details for these people yet, but you can purchase mailing lists from list brokers. There are many companies like this that provide targeted marketing. For example, you can purchase lists of book buyers, business starters, doctors, music buyers and working mothers.

¤ Conduct a telemarketing campaign. Once again, you can buy filtered lists of potential customers.

¤ Conduct a publicity campaign to promote your brand. While not directly targeted at procrastinators, these potential customers may notice your campaign and therefore remember your brand when they do finally get around to making a purchase.

Your message for the procrastinators

At this level of the Preneur Marketing Hierarchy, you have to start introducing people to the benefits of your product or service, as well as the benefits of your business. For example, the procrastinator who has renovated her house but has run out of steam before she put the fence up needs to be reminded by your ad that a new fence will:

¤ increase security

¤ increase privacy

¤ make the home more attractive

¤ increase the value of the property

¤ keep the children and the dog in (or out).

You don't actually need to explain what a fence is. Once this procrastinator has been nudged in the right direction, your advertising will alert her to your great prices, wonderful service, new range of fences, and money-back guarantee if the fence falls over in the first 12 months, thereby attracting her to your business.

Ignorants

Let me firstly say that I don't mean to use the word ignorant in an insulting way. What I'm referring to is people who have no idea about your product or service, or your business. They are obviously going to be the most difficult people to sell to — but this is where most businesses play. They go straight into advertising to convince the masses that their product or service will fix a problem, but they first need to convince the marketplace that it has a problem it just isn't aware of. The procrastinators and members of the lower levels of the hierarchy know that they have a problem, so there is less inertia to overcome than there is at the ignorant level.

Reaching the ignorants

Ignorants can generally only be reached through a mass-marketing campaign: television, newspapers, magazines, the internet, direct mail and just about anything else you can think of. They are not looking for your product, and are not likely to stumble across it any time soon, so the only solution is to hit them over the head with your campaign. You will encounter the most resistance at this level, so the costs are correspondingly high (and often out of reach for many small businesses). This level of marketing should only be used when you have exhausted the lower, cheaper levels of the hierarchy.

A side benefit of publicity is reaching this level very cost effectively. These people read and it's often newspapers that bring a problem to light for people. So if your business is computer security, write a press release about how dangerous it can be to have a computer system that isn't properly protected, especially for businesses. If you are interviewed as a result of this, and some ignorants read the article, you have just told these people about a problem they didn't know they had, and they have also learnt about you and your business at the same time. And all at virtually no cost to you. Fantastic!

Your message for the ignorants

You must explain to this group what your product is and how it will benefit them, and then you can tell them why they should choose your business. As a good example, a friend of mine recently bought a hybrid car. I have never considered a hybrid car and would take some convincing to do so. I know very little about them except that they have both an electric motor and a petrol engine, and therefore use a lot less petrol. My initial reaction was that I can now probably outrun my friend's new car on my skateboard. To convince me otherwise, Toyota or Holden or Ford would need to run an advertising campaign showing that hybrid cars are cheaper to run, better for the environment, and just the same as a normal car in every other way. And they'll have to do this on television or in the papers, because I'm not going to do an internet search on hybrid cars. Once I've seen the ad ten times and started to become aware that I'm driving a petrol guzzler that's destroying the planet, they will then need to persuade me to buy from them, which is an altogether different message. So, ignorants must first be told what a hybrid car is and how it will benefit them, and they then need to be persuaded to buy from a particular manufacturer.

Using the Preneur Marketing Hierarchy

The aim of the Preneur Marketing Hierarchy is to give you a structure to help you target your marketing, ensuring you match your message and your approach to the people you are trying to reach and so receive the best value for your advertising dollar.

To maximise your marketing budget, start at the bottom of the hierarchy where you will encounter the least resistance. This is especially important when you are just starting out and probably don't have much cash. Of course you may not have any customers (or friends) when you start up, but start as close to the bottom of the hierarchy as you can.

Your aim is to push customers *down* the hierarchy, so you want the searchers to become callers and the procrastinators to become searchers. Only once you have systems in place for a group should you move up to the next level. Also, keep in mind that you don't have to make it to the top of the hierarchy. If you have systems in place for the first three levels and business is booming, don't feel as though you have to keep moving up the hierarchy.

Use direct mail to get started and expand your business. It is more focused and is one of the cheapest advertising methods available. Buy lists to target your most likely customers. Once your business starts to expand, mass media can be used to attract more people, because people who were targeted through other methods are now customers. As your business grows you can use a combination of methods. When your product develops into a commodity then, and only then, do you use institutional advertising such as branding and the type of adverts that most large companies use, such as billboards and televisions ads. Don't simply use one advertising method or approach for each group—think about what each needs and prepare accordingly. For example, have a different direct-mail sales letter for your existing customers and for the ignorants.

The AIDA principle

Once you have used the Preneur Marketing Hierarchy to figure out how you are going to reach your market, it is important to design an attractive and appealing advertisement. You must be able to catch people's eye, hold their attention and then make them take action. Telling people about your product is one thing but motivating them to take action and purchase from you is another.

There are a number of ways to design an ad. One of the most commonly used theories is the AIDA principle. AIDA stands for attention, interest, desire, action. This principle can help you design an effective ad. Let's take a closer look at this concept.

If you're trying to persuade people to do something, or buy something, it seems to me you should use their language, the language in which they think.

David Ogilvy — advertising expert

Attention

Whether you are using direct mail, advertising in a shopping mall or on radio or placing a promo in the local paper, the first aim of your ad is to attract attention. People must notice it. Keep in mind that it may appear among lots of other advertisements—what will you do to make sure that people notice your ad and not your competitors'?

One of the best ways to get people to read your ad is to use an attention-grabbing headline. For example, 'You are paying too much for your insurance!' is more likely to hook a reader than 'Cheap insurance'. And 'Cut your heating bills by 25 per cent!' is more attention grabbing than 'Efficient heaters available'. At the time of writing, ANZ is advertising credit cards with the headline 'Irate about your credit card interest rate?' This is effective because most people will say 'yes' to that. And *The Age* is advertising its Drive section with the heading 'Win $100 worth of petrol today'. Who doesn't want to win $100 worth of petrol? Both of these headlines instantly engage the reader and entices him or her to read on.

When coming up with your headline consider your USP. Can you use it in your headline? If you have a good USP, it should be perfect for this. For example, 'Cheapest home insurance in Melbourne, guaranteed'. That's a USP and a headline in one.

You can also attract attention by using bright colours and a large, bold headline and by using words such as new, easy, save, best, amazing, fantastic, money, secret, proven, revolutionary, exclusive and outstanding.

The attention section needs to be adapted depending on which level of the hierarchy you are targeting. If you are selling to people you already have a relationship with, a headline like 'Try our new faster and more secure anti-virus software' would work, but, if you are targeting an ignorant, your headline will need to communicate the benefits of your 'industry'—for example, 'Our anti-virus software could save you a fortune by protecting your business'. A single headline will not reach all levels of the hierarchy.

Interest

Once people have noticed your ad, you can maintain their interest in a number of ways.

Explain how your product or service will benefit them or solve a problem that they have. For example, don't say in your ad, 'Our new blender has a 1000-volt motor with 37 different speeds and the latest complicated technology'. Instead try: 'The technology in our new blender will enable you to enjoy those yummy fruit smoothies in half the time'. People don't really care about the technology itself—they care about how it will help them. Use the word 'you'—'This is how our product or service will benefit *you*'.

Use testimonials from satisfied customers, or an image that demonstrates how your product is used or how the customer will benefit. Another good way to maintain interest is to include statistics—for example, the number of people already using your product or service, the amount of money that can be saved, or how much more quickly a task can be accomplished.

Can you link your advertising to events or dates? For example, during the 2006 World Cup, soccer was used to advertise *everything,* even products and services that had nothing to do with soccer.

Desire

The next step is to increase desire. What will make people desperately want your product or service? Find an angle that increases desirability and your sales will increase too. This can be done in a variety of ways, including:

¤   Scarcity—get it now before we run out—limited offer.

¤   Price—on sale until the end of the month.

¤   Popularity—product or service already used by 500 000 people around Australia.

◻ Bonuses—buy now and get a free set of steak knives or buy two and get one free.

◻ Images—for a travel agency, people sitting on a beach in Fiji drinking cocktails.

Action

Make sure the potential customer knows what to do next. You *must* make it easy for people to reach you. This is the most important step, so make sure you include your contact details in all of your advertising. Depending on your product or service, you could even include an order form that can be mailed or faxed in. It is no good attracting interest or having an eye-catching ad if people don't follow up and contact you. The aim of advertising is to make sales. Here are some examples of effective calls to action:

Download:

To download a free report on how to test and monitor your advertising, go to <www.preneurmarketing.com. au/testing.php>.

◻ Call us now to order.

◻ Call us now to make an appointment.

◻ Call us now and we'll come to you.

◻ Email us to receive a free sample.

◻ Go to our website for more information or to sign up.

◻ We're open every day of the week—come and see us.

$ $ $ $ $

No matter what your product or service is, you are in the business of marketing. More than anything else, you must generate interest in your product or service using publicity and advertising, and then turn this interest into sales. Having the best widgets in the world will not guarantee you sales. *Letting people know* that you have the best widgets in the world is what results in sales. A great product with poor marketing will be easily outsold by an average product with good marketing. Make sure that you give your marketing the attention it deserves.

If you don't think advertising works, think of all the millions
of people who think yoghurt tastes good.
Bob Orben — writer

Chapter 12

From imagination to...

influence factors

> The only way to influence someone is to find out what
> they want, and show them how to get it.
> **Dale Carnegie — US author and lecturer**

Key points

¤ You can use the six principles of influence to encourage
   people to buy from you.

¤ Incorporate these principles into your marketing and your
   business systems.

¤ Each approach can be adapted to suit your business, product
   or service.

The aim of your publicity and marketing is to influence people
to buy from you and in this chapter we are going to examine the
psychology behind influence. I am not saying trick, deceive or
scam—I am saying influence, by which I mean encourage people
to see the benefits of your product or service. Robert Cialdini is
a professor of psychology and he has written a great book called
Influence: The Psychology of Persuasion. I am going to discuss
Cialdini's six 'weapons of influence', how I used them in the MCG

venture and how these can be used by any budding entrepreneur to increase sales. You may be aware of some of these but this chapter will detail the psychology behind why these techniques are used. Once you have an understanding of the psychology, you can adapt and use these theories in other creative ways.

The six weapons are:

¤ Social proof—if others have bought this product it must be good.

¤ Liking—people are more likely to buy from a person or business they like.

¤ Authority—people will be influenced by an authority figure.

¤ Scarcity—people are more likely to buy if something is scarce.

¤ Reciprocation—people will be influenced if you give them something.

¤ Commitment and consistency—if a person makes a commitment to you or your business, he or she will be more likely to buy from you.

Social proof

Cialdini states that one method people use to 'determine what is correct is to find out what other people think is correct'. He calls this 'social proof', and it can affect everything we do in life—how fast we drive, what movies we see, what clothes we buy, what restaurants we go to.

Advertisers and marketers commonly use this theory in an attempt to influence people to buy their products or services, and with good reason—it works! An ad might include the statistic: 'Already used by 300 000 Australians'. Without even naming a product, most of us would instinctively and subconsciously react with, 'Well, it must be good then'. We automatically assume that

300 000 people wouldn't have bought a product that was no good. Publishers use this all the time when they put a sticker on a book that says 'Over 100 000 copies sold'. (Let's hope I can get one of those stickers!) This doesn't say anything about the quality of the book but publishers know it will help to sell more copies because of the effect that social proof has on consumers.

Another way to obtain social proof is through testimonials from existing customers. People believe testimonials because this is what your customers are saying about you, not what you are saying about yourself—sounds a lot like the halo effect doesn't it? I use testimonials wherever I can in my marketing and on <www.preneurmarketing.com.au>. Did you read the advance praise at the start of this book?

Social proof can also be achieved through celebrity endorsements. People want to be seen wearing the same watch as Brad Pitt or using the same make-up as Claudia Schiffer. This is due to the two following perceptions:

¤ 'If Brad uses it, it must be good!'

¤ 'I want people to see that I'm just as cool and rich and successful as Claudia.'

Of course, Brad is paid to endorse the product, and wearing the same make-up as Claudia probably won't transform the wearer into a supermodel (although my gorgeous girlfriend, who is a make-up artist, would disagree), but social proof is all about perception, not facts.

I use social proof for selling the pens made from MCG wood. On my website I have the following headline: 'Imagine the reaction you will get pulling this unique pen out during a sales presentation or imagine the thanks you will receive when you give this amazing and memorable gift to family or friends'. The message: if you buy and use this pen, people will think you're important and impressive.

The key to successful leadership today is influence, not authority.
Kenneth Blanchard — American business consultant and author

Using social proof in your business

The obvious way to use social proof is by selling a large amount of your product or service and then advertising this fact: 'Over 300 000 solar-powered toasters sold' or '1000 new subscribers every week'. The people who are buying from you are giving their endorsement to your product and this will convince your potential customers that you are selling something worthwhile. People are also comfortable being part of a crowd, even if the product turns out to be not so good: 'If the solar-powered toaster blows up, at least 300 000 other people will have the same problem and I won't feel so stupid'.

Another way to acquire social proof is to ask customers to provide you with testimonials. If you've given them good service they will be happy to do this. Put these testimonials on your website or in your ads (with the person's permission of course). This encourages potential customers to deal with you because others have been happy with your business. Testimonials can also state how you helped your customers. For example, a testimonial may read, 'I've never used internet marketing before, but Acme Internet Marketing helped me set up a website, create a Google campaign and start an email newsletter'. This will be encouraging for other potential clients who also have never used internet marketing.

A good testimonial is more than just, 'This is a great product'. If you have the room, use a few lines or even a paragraph. Have the customer clearly explain how you helped him or her and the benefits of your product or service. For example, a freelance publisher that I have worked with has the following testimonial on his website:

> Michael did the book production for my Great Australian Novel. I liked that he was careful with the writer's ego and was interested in getting the GAN onto paper, and was pleased when it looked good. I was pleased too, and others have said that the book was nice to read: comfortable font size, line length, line spacing, margins, sturdy cover, flexible paper, nice colour. These weren't things I knew about but Michael did. When the next GAN is due, I'll be talking to Michael.

Notice how it clearly spells out what was done and why the service was good. This is a good testimonial that will encourage others to use Michael's services.

It's also very important that you put a name to the testimonial, otherwise it has no credibility. If your customer does not want his or her name included, do not use the testimonial.

And no matter how tempting it may be, *don't write them yourself and put fictitious names on them.* Sooner or later somebody will find out that you have done this and your credibility will be ruined. If your customers are pleased with your business, you will have no problems getting good—real—testimonials. Once you have your testimonials, use them in both your publicity and advertising.

Once you finish reading this book I would love your feedback and testimonials; please shoot me an email at <testimonial@pre neurmarketing.com.au> with your comments—you may even be rewarded (*hint hint*).

> **Pete's tip: karma**
>
> *I am a big believer in karma. If you do a deal with a charity for liking only, I firmly believe that you will pay some sort of price down the track. However, if you are genuine in your efforts, you will receive great satisfaction and your business will benefit as well.*

Liking

The principle of liking is easy to understand—people are more likely to buy from somebody they like. This, of course, does not mean you have to become best mates with your customers. It simply means treating them in a friendly way and making a connection with them. Cialdini gives the example of the 'world's greatest car salesman' Joe Girard, whose theory is simple—he offers people just two things, a reasonable price and a person they like to buy from.

Another way this principle can be effective is if people 'like' your business. For example, if you donate money to charity, or support the local kids' sports club, or donate your services to the local school, people will see your business as caring and will therefore 'like' you more. Developing a strategic alliance with the E.J. Whitten Foundation created liking for my MCG venture, as people 'like' foundations. (This is discussed in chapter 16, which is about teamwork.) Don't, however, start doing these things just to create this liking effect, as people will know if you are being generous just to further your business interests. Take a genuine interest in helping others and let the benefits to your business be a fortunate side effect.

Using liking in your business

There is no easy way to get people to like you, especially when you may only have contact with some customers for a few minutes, but here are some obvious suggestions:

¤ Always be pleasant and approachable. Even if you're having a bad day, don't let your customers know this.

¤ Hire friendly staff.

¤ Find similarities with your clients. If a client came into my office and happened to mention she was a basketball fan, I could talk to her all day. People like sharing their interests, so see if you can find some common ground.

¤ Be cooperative. For example, if you are having trouble agreeing on a time for an appointment, offer to go and see the customer after hours.

¤ Ask for referrals. When a friend refers you to a business, you are more likely to follow this advice because you like the person. (Referrals are also a form of social proof—your existing customer is endorsing your business by recommending it, so the second person is more likely to follow the suggestion.)

Tupperware parties are an example of a business model that uses the liking principle to maximum effect. People are being sold to at a friend's house, in the middle of a group of friends, at a party arranged by a friend. This all conspires to encourage people to buy, because they trust the person who arranged the party and also because they feel a sense of obligation to help their friend's business. Can you implement a system to sell your products in a similar way?

You can also make regular donations to charities or organisations in your local area. This will foster goodwill towards you and your business. Coles, for example, has a program called 'Coles Cares', through which it supports a number of good causes.

At the time of writing, NAB is making good use of this influence factor — the most prominent headline on its website reads, 'Congratulations to the customers of the year'. NAB have apparently just won a bank of the year award but it believes its customers are the key to its success. Awwwww, aren't they nice at the NAB. I like them.

> You will make more friends in a week by getting yourself interested in other people than you can in a year by trying to get other people interested in you.
>
> **Arnold Bennett**

Authority

The influence of authority comes about because people are inclined to listen to people they see as experts or authority figures. We see this every day. If you walk into the hardware store, you assume the person behind the counter with the overalls on knows what she is talking about, and you'll quite happily take her advice about how to repair your gate or pave the driveway or build a treehouse. You don't ask her what her experience is or how long she has worked at the store — she's behind the counter, she's the expert. I know an accountant who has written a few accounting books. He told me that after he began displaying these in his office, he noticed a significant reduction in the number of questions people asked him! The authority portrayed by the books meant people were more comfortable taking his advice, which resulted in fewer queries 'questioning' his theories or advice — they simply trusted what he said.

Authority also comes from media coverage (which you will get as a result of your great publicity) and endorsements. The MCG venture was covered in Eddie McGuire's *Herald Sun* column—this gave a sense of authority to my business. Eddie is an expert on all things football, and I appeared on his page, so therefore I must know what I'm doing.

Another example is Readings bookstores in Melbourne. Readings promotes its authority by having authors speak in the stores and by being the official bookseller for the Melbourne Writers' Festival. It also creates reciprocation (explained in more detail later in this chapter) because some of the in-store events are free.

Using authority in your business

People will be more easily persuaded when they see that you have expertise and are knowledgeable about the product or service you are selling. This must be genuine though, so know your products and services thoroughly, and make sure you are prepared for any questions or problems that may arise.

You can maximise this effect by earning a reputation as an expert in your field so that people have heard about you before they contact you. Include in your press release details of your experience, and any major successes you have had. This might result in an interview, which instantly gives you authority. If you develop a reputation as an expert, journalists will contact you when they need information or a comment. You can also write newspaper or magazine articles, or a book. These days, if you can't find a publisher it's easy to self-publish a book. Starting a newsletter is also a good way to convey authority.

You could also approach celebrities or well-known people to see if they would be interested in endorsing or supporting your venture, so that you benefit from their authority. This will be difficult while you are small but as your business gathers momentum you may have more luck.

Publicity also helps with authority—once you are published or quoted in an article you are perceived as an expert and you can use this in any later marketing endeavours to create authority.

Scarcity

Cialdini writes that people seem to be more motivated by the thought of losing or missing out on something than by the thought of gaining something. People are encouraged to act by the possibility that they might miss out on something good.

We've all experienced this. If you saw that a product that you wanted was on sale for the next 12 months, you wouldn't race down to the store. But if it's advertised as being on sale until stocks run out, you might jump in the car right away. People are attracted by scarcity because it implies that an item is more valuable. This is also a form of social proof in that scarcity implies that other people have bought it. This principle is obvious in children from the youngest age — the best way to get a child to want something is to tell her that she can't have it.

I applied this principle when selling the 'G by making the frames

> **Pete's tip: using the principles**
>
> *These six principles of influence are great for attracting new customers, but they can also be used to keep existing ones. Look at the Preneur Marketing Hierarchy to see how you can apply these principles to each level.*

in numbered limited editions and promoting this in my advertising. If a person buys a frame numbered '16 of 50', he or she knows that only 49 other people have the same frame. This creates exclusivity and increases the frame's value.

Using scarcity in your business

Scarcity is probably the easiest of these concepts to include in your business systems. You can easily create limited editions of your products. For example, at the time of writing, Ford is offering a special edition Territory with $3850 worth of extras for free, only for a limited time. This implies scarcity in two ways: 'special edition' (not many people will have it) and 'for a limited time' (only people who are quick will get one). Honda has a 'Once a Year Day Sale', where it offers discounts and bonuses such as free registration. It doesn't get much more scarce than once a year.

You can create limited editions whatever you are selling. If you sell clothes, have 100 T-shirts signed by a football player near grand final time. If you sell computers, create 50 packages with a larger, more expensive monitor than you usually provide, throw in some free software and call it a 'limited edition deluxe package'. Voila! Scarcity! Include this package in your advertising to encourage people to visit your store or website, and if people don't buy the limited edition package they may still buy something else from you. You can also do this with services businesses. If your business is walking dogs, give away a free lead to the first 30 people who book your service at the start of a new year. If you run a car wash, provide 25 per cent off for the first 50 customers every Tuesday. When customer 51 turns up and realises she has missed out, chances are she will still have her car washed anyway.

Some other ways to create scarcity are:

¤ have a sale for a limited time

¤ advertise a product with 'only 16 left'

¤ sell a limited number of tickets to a publicity event

¤ with every purchase, give away vouchers for a 5 per cent discount that must be used within the next two months

¤ advertise your products with the line 'contact us now before we run out'.

The harder something is to obtain the higher its perceived value. Scarcity is an easy concept to use in your business so incorporate it into your marketing systems. This is where structuring your business, as explained earlier, to create the 'guru at the top of the mountain' effect fits in.

At the time of writing, Crazy John's is giving away a mobile phone every 24 hours. It actually has a counter on its website counting down to when the next phone will be given away. How's that for creating a sense of scarcity — only one per day! I only have to wait 19 hours and 32 minutes to see if I've won. Better put on some coffee ...

If you want to succeed you should strike out on new paths,
rather than travel the worn paths of accepted success.
John Rockefeller

Reciprocation (givers get)

The principle behind reciprocation is to create a sense of indebtedness that may produce a positive response when the result may otherwise have been negative. If you give something to people, they feel obliged to give something back.

You don't have to look far to see marketers using this approach. One of the most common promotional tools is to give something away for free. We've all been approached in a shopping centre by a person giving away free samples of food, shampoo or toothpaste. This has two effects. Firstly, we get to try the product, and if we like it we may buy it. Secondly, we start to feel a sense of obligation towards the company that gave us something for free (not always consciously), so next time we are in the supermarket, this might encourage us to choose that brand. These effects are exactly the aim of such promotions.

It is also common these days for businesses to give away free information on their websites, such as a report or an article. This attracts people to the site and if they find the information useful it will create a feeling of obligation to buy from the company. You can also give people a discount or a bonus gift the first time they buy from you.

Using reciprocation in your business

Give something away! Put a useful report on your website, create a small sample version of your product and give it away at train stations or give away vouchers to use your service for free the first time. This will attract people to your business and will also make them feel a sense of obligation towards you once they have taken up your offer.

Tupperware parties are a great example of reciprocation. The host of the party provides lunch, drinks and biscuits during the presentation, which instils reciprocation (often subconsciously) and encourages people to buy. Friends of mine base the presents they buy for formal functions, such as 21st birthday parties or engagements and weddings, on the value of what the party hosts would have spent on them in catering—that's reciprocation at its best!

Commitment and consistency

People act in line with their commitments. Cialdini states that we have a 'nearly obsessive desire to be (and to appear) consistent with what we have already done'. This is the theory behind those competitions where you have to state in '25 words or less' why you like a particular product. The rationale is that if you make people write down why they like your business, they will then subconsciously want to keep their word, so next time they have to choose they will select your product.

This principle means that people will feel a sense of obligation to you if they have told you they like your product or that they would find it useful. Once people make a commitment, especially in public, they will usually make an effort to stick to it.

Using commitment and consistency in your business

You can use the type of competition mentioned above to create a sense of commitment to your business. Run a competition where entrants have to state in 30 words or fewer why your frozen yoghurt is better than all the other frozen yoghurts on the market. This makes them think about why they like your product, and will also encourage them to buy from you because they feel they have decided that your yoghurt is the best and they will want to be consistent with this. Use the entries as testimonials—with permission, of course.

You now know the reasoning behind running such a competition, rather than just doing it because you've seen others do it—which is never a path to success. Here's an example of a business that *doesn't* appear to understand why these types of competitions are run. At the time of writing, a book publisher is having a competition that asks readers to do the following: 'In 25 words or less, describe your favourite place to read in winter and why'. What's the point in that? Why not create positive feelings towards the books you publish? For example, 'Describe in 25 words or less your favourite book published by us'. This is an example of a business using a promotional tool without really understanding why. Don't make the same mistake!

You can also use this principle when talking to clients. As you discuss with them the benefits of what you are selling, get an agreement from them each step of the way. Don't just bombard them with information. So, if you are trying to sell a mobile phone, you would say: 'This phone lasts 20 per cent longer than most others on each charge. Would you find that useful?' Then, 'This phone can also play music through headphones. Do you think you could use that?' And so on. Then, if the customer has replied yes to all or most of these, when it is time to say 'Yes, I'll take it', they have almost talked themselves into buying the phone by agreeing that they would find the benefits useful. This approach will give you more success than simply reading a list of features to the customer.

Use the concept of commitment and consistency to encourage people to make a written or verbal commitment to your company. They are then more likely to purchase from you.

Influence and the hierarchy

Keep in mind the Preneur Marketing Hierarchy and use these approaches to keep existing customers as well as to attract new ones. The six influence principles can be used with every level of the hierarchy.

However, influencing people at different levels of the hierarchy will require different approaches. For example, use the principle of reciprocation and give current customers (the bottom of the hierarchy) 10 per cent off every fifth purchase. Or, try using the principle of scarcity and tell callers (the next level up) that you can give them a good deal but only if they come to see you today.

The ethics of influence

Pete's tip:
benefits versus features

Keep in mind the difference between a feature and a benefit. The feature is the phone lasts longer on each charge, the benefit is you can go away for the weekend and not have to take your charger. Always sell on the benefits, not the features.

If you use these tools—and that is all they are—unethically or dishonestly, not only will you be caught out but karma will get you as well. I would never advocate trying to deceive or manipulate customers. Using the power of influence is just another way that you can encourage people to buy from you, by adding value to your products or services and telling people why your business is great. It does not involve tricks or chicanery.

Chapter 13

From imagination to...

clicks and portals

When I took office, only high energy physicists had ever heard of what is called the world wide web ... Now even my cat has its own page.

Bill Clinton

Key points

¤ It is *essential* to use the internet in your business.

¤ The internet is not a magic money-making tool — you must still use sound business practices in the cyber world.

¤ Use your website and eBay to sell your products or services.

¤ Use email to communicate with your customers.

These days having a clicks and portals store is just as common as having a bricks and mortar store. You can market and sell absolutely anything on the internet and achieve a global audience without leaving your desk. There is simply no other way to reach a market this size and at a comparatively small cost. Whatever your business is, you must make use of this immensely powerful tool.

Don't get e-fooled

I'm going to open this chapter with a few words about some common internet traps people fall in to. The first—and biggest—trap to avoid is believing that you are running an *internet* business. Unless you are actually selling internet-related products or services, you are *not* running an internet business. Amazon.com is not an internet business—it's an online store that sells books, music and many other items. eBay is not an internet business—it's an auction business that transacts over the internet.

In order to make the most of using the internet in your business, you must realise that it is just another channel through which you can distribute and sell your products, the same as having a shop in a mall or conducting a mail-out. Yes, many businesses have made millions selling over the internet but to do this you must not forget the business you are in. When Amazon was just starting up, it still had to think about how to best reach book buyers, which books to sell, how to manage delivery and all those other issues that also need to be considered when opening in a shopping mall. Amazon is a retail bookstore, not an internet business.

I think that many people forgot this during the tech-share boom a few years ago—everything became an *internet* business and traditional business fundamentals were thrown out the Windows (get it?). But the new economy proved to be a lot like the old one—businesses with poor planning, weak financials and dodgy fundamentals were sent rapidly broke, no matter how much hype surrounded them.

This leads us to the second internet trap: don't think that you can simply set up a website and you will instantly be flooded with more sales than you can handle. This is very far from the truth. Even with a fantastic website your business will still live or die based on your publicity, marketing, quality of service and all those other things that determine business success. The internet is a very powerful tool but it is still just one of many aspects of your business that you have to get right to succeed.

Okay, now for the good stuff. Let's have a look at what you can do with that mass of interconnected computers we call the internet. According to *Reader's Digest* (July 2005), Australians spent $617 million buying products on the net. This is the third-largest market behind the US and UK. Make sure you are getting some of this action!

Your business website

Most people start incorporating the internet into their business by setting up a website for the venture (also sometimes called a home page). A website is not optional these days—it is as essential as a telephone or fax machine. You can set up a basic site for a few hundred dollars or spend tens of thousands of dollars creating a site that NASA would be proud of.

A website is a powerful tool because it instantly gives you access to a worldwide audience, and people can find out about—and buy from—your business 24 hours a day, seven days a week. It is also great value for money in terms of the number of people you can reach and the amount of information you can provide.

You must first decide what part your website will play in your business. Will you sell exclusively online (like Amazon) or will the website augment your other sales channels (like most businesses)? If your business is going to exist completely in the digital world you will need an appropriate site. You must have it professionally designed (don't do it yourself), and it must have all the features people expect these days, such as a shopping cart, secure payment, a good search facility, images and comprehensive information on your products or

Pete's tip: .au?

When you are registering a domain name, you will have a choice between .com and .com.au. Think carefully about what is appropriate for your business. If you are aiming to sell internationally, go for .com. If being identified as Australian is important to your business, choose .com.au.

services. If you are using the website as one of many sales channels, you still must have a good site but you can probably get away with something a bit simpler (and therefore cheaper).

When selling the 'G, I set up a website to promote and sell the frames: <www.sportinglimitededitions.com>. This was just one of many marketing tools that I used. This website now features the MCG pens, with information on the timber and how the pens were made and of course an order form. On Hold Advertising's website is one of its major marketing tools. It includes detailed information about the company, its products and services, testimonials, FAQs, pricing details, contact details and samples for prospective customers to listen to.

Here are some tips for creating an effective business website that will help increase your sales:

- Create pages that load quickly. This means don't go over the top with images or tonnes of text. Don't make people wait for a page to load, because they won't. We've all heard about how short people's attention … spans … something about … websites … these days … are …

- Provide free and useful information. This gives people a reason to come to your site.

- Update your site regularly. There's nothing more annoying for your customers than an out-of-date website. And you don't want people emailing you about the sale that ended six months ago. If you update regularly and include useful information, you give people a reason to come back.

- Make navigation easy, with clearly labelled and logical links. This is where a web professional will be able to help.

- Provide images of your products or services.

- Provide contact details, including an address or phone number. This gives your business substance in a virtual world.

- Check the compatibility of your site. This is often overlooked. There are many different software and hardware combinations available. Your website must be easy to access for everybody, not just Windows users running Explorer. A web professional will be able to help you with this.

¤ If your site is purely sales/lead-generation based, guide the viewer through the sales process (page) just like you would if you were selling face to face.

So they have the internet on computers now?

Homer Simpson

Not lost in cyber space

Danger! Danger! Danger, Will Robinson! You're not just going to start up a website and wait for the orders to flood in, are you? Let me tell you with 100 per cent certainty that this won't work. Just as if you had opened up a bricks and mortar store, when you start up a website you must let people know about it so that they can find it. Let's have a look at some of the ways you can do this.

Search engine keyword advertising

If you want to make sure that your website appears at or near the top of the results list when people perform a web search, you'll have to create an advertising campaign with the search engines. Otherwise you might end up on page 23 and nobody will ever find you—most people only go three or four pages deep. Two of the most popular search engines are Google and Yahoo! and both offer advertising based on keyword searches.

Both of these work in a similar way. Using keyword tools on the site you can select search terms that you would like to link your ad to. The search site will give you statistics on how often that term is used. Once you have created your ad (which usually comprises a heading and a few lines of text), you then make a bid for how much you are willing to pay for that term. The position of your ad will depend on how your bid compares with other bids. For example, if you search for 'messages on hold' (our most searched keyword) you will see my company's ad near the top of the sponsored searches on Google (see figure 13.1). This means my company currently has one of the highest bids for the term 'on hold advertising'. If somebody placed a higher bid for this term, my ad would appear second on the list and so on if more higher bids were placed for this term.

Figure 13.1: On Hold Advertising's ad on Google

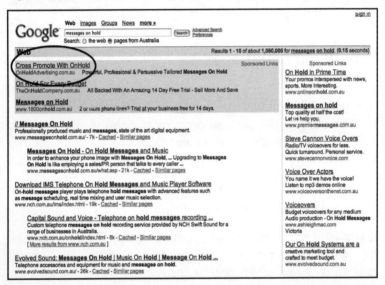

As with all types of auctions, the terms that are more in demand will cost more to bid on. A little-used search term might cost you 10¢, while a popular term might cost $10.00. A great feature of these systems is that you are bidding for *clicks*, not *impressions*. Each time your ad appears is an impression, but you don't pay for this. You only pay when somebody clicks on your ad and goes through to your site. This feature allows you to easily and affordably split-test adverts—split testing is when you simultaneously test two adverts or headlines to see which one gets the larger response. Compare this with traditional offline advertising, such as print magazines—here you are only paying for 'impressions' and the response or effectiveness has nothing to do with the costs.

If you used the keyword fish-finder technique in chapter 3, you should already have a good idea of the keywords that you would like to use. If not, you should do this before setting up a keywords campaign.

Here are some suggestions for making the most of your search-engine advertising:

¤ Using the keyword tools, find out how much current advertisers are paying for search terms. This will give you an idea of the more profitable terms.

¤ Use the search keywords in your ad to show the searcher the relevance of your site.

¤ Carefully select your keywords to attract the right people to your site. It is better to bid higher on a few carefully selected terms than to spread your bids across a large number of less-relevant terms.

¤ Test and monitor your ad. Change the headline and the copy to see what attracts the most click-thrus to your site. Remember to alter only one thing at a time so that you can see what causes the biggest change to the response rate. Once you've found what attracts the most potential customers, stick with it. (Google can monitor and compare your ads for you.)

¤ You don't have to send people to your home page. Choose the page on your site that provides the most appropriate information and link your ad to that page.

Keep in mind the Preneur Marketing Hierarchy. At this level you are trying to reach the searchers, so ask yourself what information they would require and what you can put in your ad to attract them.

I think it's fair to say that personal computers have become the most empowering tool we've ever created. They're tools of communication, they're tools of creativity, and they can be shaped by their user.

Bill Gates

Search-engine optimisation

The above section addressed ways to improve your *paid* search-engine advertising but there are also things you can do to improve the ranking of your website in the *non-paid* section of the search results. This is called 'search-engine optimisation'. I would not suggest this as an alternative to a paid campaign as it is much harder to work your way to the top of the list, but if you can't afford to pay at the beginning or you just wish to improve your chances of being found, the following suggestions will be useful.

To optimise your website so that it achieves a good search ranking:

¤ Suggest your own site to the search engines. (This doesn't actually help your ranking but the first step is to get listed.)

¤ Ensure that your website contains useful content and regularly use keywords on your site that people are likely to use to find your site. (Refer back to chapter 3 for how to research keywords.)

¤ Add your keywords to your meta tags. Don't try this at home. If you don't know what a meta tag is, you need a web professional to help. Let's just say that doing this will make you stand out more to the search engines.

¤ Give your web pages compelling titles. The title is what appears as the link in the search results—this is what people actually click on to reach your site. Make it enticing!

¤ Trade links with other sites. Having links going in and out of your site helps to make you more 'visible' on the internet.

Search-engine optimisation is an ongoing project, not something you can do once and forget about. To maintain your ranking you must keep up with the search terms people are using, what your competitors are doing and how many clicks you are attracting.

Search-engine optimisation is not as reliable as placing a sponsored listing. If you can afford it, I suggest placing some paid listings. If your campaign is well designed, the ads will more than pay for themselves.

Banner ads

Banner ads are like mini internet billboards that direct people to your site. You don't have to look far to find them on the internet. The best way to maximise the amount of traffic you receive from a banner ad is to place it on a site that has relevance to yours. For example, if you sell ski gear, see if you can place a banner ad on a ski resort's website. Or if you sell car accessories, place an ad on car dealership websites.

As with the keyword advertising, banner ads are often placed on a 'cost per click' basis. This means that you only pay for the ad each time somebody clicks through to your website. Use the AIDA principles explained in chapter 11 to create an attention-grabbing ad (but remember that you don't have much room in a banner ad).

Pete's tip:
If you visit my links page at <www.preneurmarketing.com.au/freeresources_link.php> you can apply to be added to my links page. Or if you have a site of your own and wish to link to me, visit <www.preneurmarketing.com.au/freesources_gotalink.php>.

Links

A good way to inform people about your site at no cost is to trade links with businesses that are operating in your field but are not competitors; so, you put a link to their sites on your site and vice versa. You could even do this as a recommendation. So, if you sell motorbikes, you could recommend a garage that specialises in servicing bikes and it can recommend people to you who wish to purchase a bike. Make sure it's easy for people to link to you. Create a separate page on your site dedicated to helping people link back to you—the easier something is, the better.

eBay

eBay <www.ebay.com.au> is an example of a great web-based business that operates exclusively online. I'm not going to explain what eBay is because you must have been living under a rock in a cave at the top of a very high mountain if you don't know. But we are going to look at how to use eBay in your business.

eBay has created some of the most incredible entrepreneurial success stories in the history of commerce ...

<www.entrepreneur.com>

eBay is a great entrepreneurial story in itself. It started in San Francisco; one of the founders wanted to build a site for his girlfriend to give Pez dispenser collectors (yes, apparently they exist) an avenue to trade and sell. He also believed that an auction system was the best way to establish fair market value for items. He added a small section to his existing website called AuctionWeb. When he saw how enthusiastically people bought and sold the Pez dispensers, the idea for a wider ranging auction site was born. Of course, like many of these stories this element of the start-up has turned into legend, but it was a factor in eBay getting started. (Okay, so maybe I did explain it a bit ... but it's a good story, right?)

It has grown so much that some people use eBay as the sole distribution channel for their businesses. (Notice how I didn't say some people 'run an eBay business'.) The site now has services to cater specifically for businesses. eBay instantly opens you up to an Australia-wide or worldwide audience, it costs nothing to register and you can set your own trading terms (within the eBay rules, of course). As for prices, eBay operates on an auction system, so you set your minimum prices and (hopefully) watch them go up from there.

You could run your business exclusively through the site, or use it as a complement to your other sales channels. I believe that every business should use eBay in some way; it is an easy, low-cost way to promote and sell your products. I sold a lot of the unframed MCC carpet on eBay and I also sold some frames this way. It wasn't the focus of my business or marketing but it provided another income stream that required very little effort.

Even if you decide to sell mainly through eBay, I suggest having your own website as well. This gives you another marketing channel and also enables you to provide more information to your customers than you can on eBay.

eBay is designed for people selling products but it is possible (though probably more difficult) to sell services as well. Perhaps you could come up with a service package that you sell exclusively through eBay. It's a great business system to set up and it leverages your time. It is almost automatic (which is a great advantage of many internet businesses). Once you set it up, all you have to do is wait for the orders to arrive and send out the item. You can set up automatic payment and you usually don't have to deal with the customer at all, so it's a very efficient way to sell. This is why I believe eBay is essential for all businesses.

You can offer a 'no-frills' version of your product on eBay. For example, if you sell fancy coffee machines, you could also sell some more basic machines over eBay to open up another market. If you do this, it is essential that your eBay business is branded differently. You can't build a high-quality brand while selling discount items on eBay.

Getting started on eBay

Have a look around eBay and get to know it. It is free to browse the site, and there is help available for people getting started. There are also many books about starting an eBay business. See how it works, what people are selling and what your competition will be. Become familiar with eBay and how the auction system works before you start selling.

Once you are familiar with the site and have opened a seller's account, you must then decide how you are going to incorporate it into your business. Are you going to sell full-time through eBay, or will you create an automated system where you just list a few items to generate some extra income? You can also choose auction-style listings, sell at a fixed price or open an eBay store.

Once you've decided how you are going to use eBay, you should run some tests. List different items with different styles of ads and at different prices. Also, try listing packages of products in different combinations. Watch the activity to see which methods attract the most attention and the highest prices, and use this information to set up your business.

Automate your eBay selling as much as possible. Set up automatic payment and a customer service email address. You can even buy software that will manage your listings and auctions for you.

As with all aspects of your business, there will be some trial and error. But whatever your product, eBay can either be your main source of income or a low-maintenance extra income stream.

Customer relationship management via email

As the term suggests, customer relationship management (CRM) is all about how you deal with your customers, and many businesses these days are using the internet and email for this function. CRM includes providing customer service, handling payments and complaints, tracking transactions, providing information to customers and keeping track of customers.

Having an email-based CRM system can be beneficial to your business because it is a highly efficient way to stay in touch with your clients. You can answer their queries, notify them about upcoming sales and send out a regular newsletter.

Here are some suggestions:

¤ Have a customer service email address. This is convenient for your customers because they can contact you after hours, and it is highly efficient for you because you can set aside
20 minutes a couple of times a day to respond to emails, rather than have the phone ringing all day. Mine is: <customer service@preneurmarketing.com.au>.

¤ Set up an email 'auto-responder' to acknowledge emails as soon as they have been received, and have an email policy that states all email inquiries will be answered within a certain time.

¤ Set up software that automatically signs people up to your email newsletter and sends it out automatically, personally addressed to the recipient. All you have to do is add the content for each edition.

¤ Set up an email alert system that automatically contacts your customers when you have a sale or special offer. You can have different lists to target people who inquired about a certain product or service. Keep in mind how these people fit into the Preneur Marketing Hierarchy.

¤ Create different email addresses so that inquiries are sent directly to the appropriate person. Have a backup person to answer these queries for each address in case the primary person is away.

¤ Have email addresses with auto-responders for certain types of inquiries. For example, have a 'new accounts' email address—for example, <newaccounts@mybusiness.com.au>—that automatically sends out the forms needed to set up an account with your business and any other essential information. No human action required!

¤ Create a list of standard email responses for frequently asked questions.

Your website is also part of your CRM. It is useful to have a detailed 'help' or 'frequently asked questions' section on your site to help people solve their own problems without having to contact you. This is better for you and the customer. You could also write a useful report. Separate it into five parts and set up an automatic delivery system that will send it out once a month after people sign up, or make it a downloadable e-book on your website. If you create an e-book, you instantly become an author, so use this 'authority' in your publicity—it's amazing how it all ties in together!

Software is available to help you with your internet-based CRM and you should automate the process as much as possible. Keeping customers happy is vital to the success of your business, so put in the time and effort to develop good customer relationship systems.

Email marketing

Email marketing can be a powerful way to advertise to your clients. You can send out regular email 'broadcasts' notifying your customers of sales or new products, provide useful information with a newsletter and include special offers. You can build your own email list from people who contact your business or you can buy them from list brokers.

Here are some ways you can maximise your email marketing:

Pete's tip: no spam!

Whatever you do, don't spam. Emailing marketing material to people who have had no contact with your company will generate lots of annoyed people and no sales, and will make you look like an amateur (which you are if you market this way).

¤ Use database software that generates personally addressed emails.

¤ Place your best offers at the top of the page so that customers see these in their preview pane when the email arrives.

¤ Have special offers only for people on your email list.

¤ Include images in your emails (but not too many or they will take a long time to download).

¤ Include a call to action (as you should in all your marketing).

¤ Make sure your newsletter is full of useful information with not too many ads.

- Include links to the appropriate landing pages on your website so that people can get the information they need quickly.

- Include surveys in your email marketing to find out more about your customers.

- Monitor your email marketing and response rates to see what works best.

There is software that can help you with your email marketing. For example, IntelliContact software <www.intellicontact.com> includes hundreds of message templates, a message scheduler, a surveying tool, a response tracker and automated subscription management—everything you need to create an automated email marketing system. (IntelliContact is another great entrepreneurial story. Ryan Allis is the CEO of Broadwick Corp., providers of IntelliContact. Over the past few years, Ryan has built three companies to $2 million or more in annual sales, two as a marketing consultant and one as CEO. And he's only 21! He was recently named in *Business Week*'s list of the 'Top 25 Entrepreneurs Under 25'.)

Download:

For a free comprehensive report on email marketing go to <www.preneurmarketing. com.au/emailmarketing.php>

Customer-friendly email lists

To make sure you don't upset your customers, only send them email marketing material if they know their name has been placed on a list. Make your lists 'opt in' (people have to choose to be added) rather than 'opt out' (people have to elect *not* to be included). Your mailing list will probably be smaller but it will be more targeted because you know the recipients are interested. You will achieve a better response rate and won't upset clients who didn't realise their names had been added.

Also, make it easy for people to unsubscribe from your list. Include an obvious unsubscribe web link or email address in all of your marketing emails.

Our success is a direct result of knowing how to market a brand
and having the right people representing the brand.

Greg Norman

Paypal

People will expect you to accept credit card payments. Paypal <www.
paypal.com.au> is a very useful online payment system that allows
you to accept credit card payments through its website without
having to set up credit card merchant
facilities. It's cheaper and easier to set
up than a merchant account with a
bank and there are services available
that have no ongoing fees—you
simply pay a small commission on
transactions. You can set up a Paypal
system linked to your own website,
or you can use email payments where
you email an invoice to customers
and they go to the Paypal website to
make payment.

Download:

*I encourage you to visit
<www.preneurmarketing.
com.au>, and make sure
you sign up for our regular
newsletter, which is
jam-packed with marketing
ideas, entrepreneurial
concepts and the latest
news from
Preneur Marketing—plus
member-only offers.*

If you are running a business that
is based solely on the internet, I do *not*
suggest using Paypal. People expect
large internet businesses to have their own secure payment facilities
on their website, like I do at <www.preneurmarketing.com.au>
and using Paypal under these circumstances would make you look
like an amateur. However, if your website is not the main focus of
your business, then using Paypal is fine. It's a cheap and easy way
for you to collect payment from your customers and it provides
them with the convenient option of credit card payment.

Affiliate programs

Affiliate programs are a great way to boost your income over the
internet. Through an affiliate program you can sell other people's
products, and also expand your own distribution by offering an

affiliate program, which allows people to market your product in return for a commission on sales. Affiliate programs are discussed further in chapter 16.

Chapter 14

From imagination to...

back-end profits

> Profit in business comes from repeat customers, customers that boast
> about your product or service, and that bring friends with them.
> **W Edwards Deming — business lecturer and consultant**

Key points

- It is easier to keep an existing customer than it is to attract a new one.

- A good back-end leverages your marketing dollars.

- Use the marketing funnel to attract people to your business and then encourage them to buy more.

- Upselling provides an added source of income at zero cost.

There are basically three ways to increase your business profits:

1 Entice new customers through the door.

2 Educate your current customers to come back more often.

3 Encourage people to spend more per purchase.

A lot of what you have read so far has been about getting new customers through the door—and this is what most businesses and marketing books focus on. In this chapter we are going to look at enticing existing customers to come back more often (the 'back-end') and we'll also have a look the third point, 'upselling' (and cross-selling).

There's a simple way to demonstrate how important these steps are. Let's assume that in your first three months of business 100 new customers walk through your door. Each of them visit your store twice and spend $100 both times. So the equation looks like this:

$$100 \times 2 \times \$100 = \$20\,000$$

Let's see what happens if you increase each of these elements by just 10 per cent:

$$110 \times 2.2 \times \$110 = \$26\,620$$

You can clearly see that a 10 per cent increase in new customers, the number of times they visit and the amount of money they spend results in a revenue increase much larger than 10 per cent. Increasing each of these by 10 per cent will result in a 33.1 per cent increase in revenue. Think about your business—it shouldn't be too difficult to increase each of these aspects by 10 per cent and of course the higher the increase the more you gain. It's leverage—again! So let's see how you can increase the second two numbers in that equation.

The point to remember about selling things is that, as well as creating atmosphere and excitement around your products, you've got to know what you're selling.
Stuart Wilde — author

The profitable back-end

Back-end sales are the sales you achieve after you have made the effort to attract a new customer. For example, if you sell computers and accessories, a new customer might come to you as a result of a mail out and buy a new computer. One month later, the same person comes back to buy more memory for his new machine.

Then the same customer comes back again to buy software and then again to buy some blank DVDs. The sale of the computer is your front-end and the sales that follow are the back-end. You can structure your business to encourage back-end sales.

Back-end profits can add enormously to the bottom line of your business. The reason is simple—you don't have to spend as much time or effort to acquire them. You will be much more profitable having repeat customers buy from you than if you have to continually attract new people to your business. Acquiring new customers can cost you a lot in terms of time and money. But once you have them, all you need to do is keep them happy and encourage them to come back, which is a lot easier—and cheaper—than attracting them in the first place.

Some companies build their whole business model around back-end sales. Let's compare Sony and Hewlett-Packard (HP). (There is not a right and wrong business model here, this is just to explain the differences.) Sony makes televisions, digital cameras, hi-fi systems, DVD players and all sorts of other electronic equipment. Its business model is to sell high-quality products and earn a reputation for excellence. As a result, Sony can charge premium prices and this is where it makes its money. HP makes computers, monitors, calculators and servers, but it is most well known for its printers. HP printers are very affordable. I have an HP multi-function colour printer that I thought was very good value at under $300. HP certainly didn't make much profit on this sale but here's where it makes its money—I spend probably another $300 per year on HP ink cartridges. HP doesn't have to convince me to choose its product, it doesn't have to find me, nor does it have to give me a discount to encourage me to buy—I already own the printer, so I *need* the HP cartridges. Think of the thousands and thousands of people all over Australia spending a few hundred dollars a year on cartridges, all at no marketing cost to HP. How's that for a back-end!

> **Pete's tip: keep your customers**
>
> *It is cheaper and easier to keep an existing customer than it is to attract a new one.*

Repeat customers give you a ready and willing market to sell to. (Think about the Preneur Marketing Hierarchy—these are the people at the bottom!) They have already bought from you before, so you know they are interested in your product or service. This makes your marketing about as focused as it can be. I sold small certificates detailing the history of the MCG with a small piece of timber for $9.90 and included a 'back-end' sales letter upselling customers to the frames containing the MCC carpet. Anybody who ordered the certificate would most likely be interested in the frames as well.

The certificates were effectively used as a lead generator. I attracted people with a cheaper product and then used the sales letter to inform them about the frames—the back-end.

On Hold Advertising offers the back-end service to clients to update their on-hold marketing messages. At particular intervals we go back to clients to ensure their marketing message is not only timely but as compelling and effective as possible for them.

Residual income

Mobile phone dealers literally give away phones. Selling the phone is not where the money is made in this business—it's in the calls. The free phone is to attract you and turn you into a customer. You walk out of the store with a shiny new phone without handing over a cent. But you've also signed up to pay $40 per month for the next 24 months! Rather than making ongoing sales to you (as with the printer cartridges), you have signed up to pay the dealer or telco for a service each month. This is called *residual income* and is a great way to make back-end profits.

Pete's tip: generate leads

Sell a cheap product, start a 'club' or a newsletter, or give something away in order to locate customers. Once they are signed up, they will become ideal candidates for back-end sales.

Companies often offer a freebie or sell at a loss in order to attract people to back-end sales or sign them up to a contract. Residual sales are a form of automated back-end sales. The phone dealer makes one sale and the back-end is built in, systemised and consistent — it's residual income. Often your back-end will be proactive in that you have to go back to the client and encourage him or her to purchase again. It's not automatic, which is the great advantage of residual income. The phone dealer only needs to make the sale once and the back-end is also taken care of in the form of the contract. Of course, the phone dealer can also still add more back-end by giving customers a brochure of all the accessories available for the phone they just bought, or a discount voucher for their next purchase or a flyer for an upcoming sale.

Adding a back-end to your business

So how do you add a back-end to your business? The first step is to start seeing your business as a back-end business. Think like HP or like a mobile phone provider. Don't think that once you have achieved the first sale, that's it. A lot of businesses look at it this way: they try to get a customer to make a sale — that's singular: *sale*. How you should be looking at it is: you make a sale to get a customer, and this customer will repeatedly come back to you and purchase more and more.

> **Pete's tip: make a sale to...**
> *You make a sale to get a customer, not get a customer to make a sale.*

Have a look at your products or services to see how they can be used to create a back-end. This doesn't necessarily mean adding something *after* your main products or services; you can add something *before* and make your main items the back-end, as I did with the certificates and the frames. It's all about attracting people with one item and then leading them on to the next.

You should also investigate how you could add residual income to your business systems. Can you sign customers up to a contract? Rent your product out? If your business is mowing lawns, perhaps you could sign clients up to a program where you go back and give the lawn a quick tidy up once a month and mow it every three months.

A good back-end offering will either be an essential requirement for what was originally purchased—such as the ink cartridges—or it will improve on, or add to, the item—such as the extra computer memory and the software. Here are a few questions that might help you find your back-end:

¤ What can you offer at a low price that will attract people to your business, secure a sale and get people to join your mailing list? I offered the certificates and small pieces of timber with the aim of finding people who might also buy the frames.

¤ What can you offer people that will help them with what they have already bought? For example, if you sell computers, can you also sell computer manuals? Or offer tutorials?

¤ Does your product require any consumables? For example, the ink in a printer or bags for a vacuum cleaner.

¤ After people have bought your product or service, what else might they be interested in? If your business is mowing lawns, you can send your clients a brochure for your landscape gardening services when you send them the bill.

¤ Can you offer products to go with your services? For example, if you are an electrician, perhaps you can back-end people into updating their smoke alarms.

¤ Can you offer upgrades for your product? People might not buy this at the time, but after owning the product for six months, they might then feel the need to make it bigger, faster, stronger, quieter...

¤ Can you offer customers a subscription to a magazine or newsletter? This can create a great back-end if people renew their subscription each year.

Selling computer software is a great way to create a back-end, as people want the upgrades that usually come out every year or two—give them a 5 per cent discount if they buy the upgrade from you. This should be enough to stop them going elsewhere.

> If your business can effectively reach its existing customer base, it will have the advantage of marketing to those who already know and like your business and its products and services.

<www.entrepreneur.com>

You can add a back-end to any business. I know a business consultant who charges $500 an hour but his marketing starts with a free report on his website. He attracts people to his website by providing free reports. He writes these himself, and they are very useful. On his site he also sells, for about $20, business books that he has written, which people discover when they go to the site to access the free reports. Then, when people receive their books in the post, they also receive a voucher for 15 per cent off his seminars, which usually cost around $250. Only when people come to his seminars does he start promoting his consultancy services.

Let's break it down:

¤ People visit his site for the free reports.

¤ They find the report useful, so they buy the book.

¤ They find the book useful, so they go to the seminar.

¤ The seminar is great, so people hire him as a consultant to their business!

From a free report to $500 an hour. He's always fully booked as a result of this expert use of the back-end. This is a great example of what is known as the 'marketing funnel'.

The marketing funnel

The marketing funnel gives you a way to get people through the door with a lead product, free report or loss leader, and then continue to upsell or back-end them into other higher priced products and services. (A loss leader, as discussed earlier, is a

195

product or service that you deliberately sell at a loss to attract people to your business, with the aim of selling more products to them once you have them.)

For the business consultant discussed earlier, the marketing funnel looks like this (I've added a 12-month consulting package at the bottom to give him another level for his funnel):

Figure 14.1: the business consultant's marketing funnel

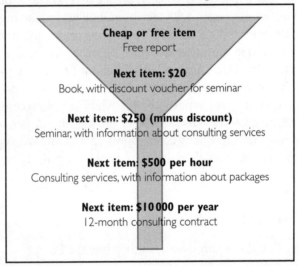

Cheap or free item
Free report

Next item: $20
Book, with discount voucher for seminar

Next item: $250 (minus discount)
Seminar, with information about consulting services

Next item: $500 per hour
Consulting services, with information about packages

Next item: $10 000 per year
12-month consulting contract

The great advantage of creating a business system like this is that it is possible to promote and market your business using a cheap or free product, which is more likely to attract customers. This can be more effective than trying to convince people to purchase the $500 per hour services first up. When people have become familiar with the cheaper products, they will see the quality and value of what is being offered, which helps to build a level of trust, so it's likely they will purchase the next item. They are spending more at each level and they are also being pushed towards the more expensive items. Customers will be more willing to pay $500 an hour for the consulting services when they reach the bottom of the funnel, which is what the business consultant is *really* trying to sell.

Many businesses have something at the top of the funnel and something at the bottom but nothing in the middle. People are less likely to jump from your free newsletter to your $1000 per day services—give them some levels in between to encourage them through the funnel.

Never be frightened to take a profit. Better in your pocket then theirs.

Michael Levy — self-help author

Databases

A great way to create a back-end is to set up a database of people who have bought from you. You can have them sign up to a newsletter, join your mailing list or become a member of your VIP club. (The main reason businesses have such clubs for their customers is to get their details, which provides a well-targeted market to sell to in the future.) Have sign-up forms in your store, send them with your invoices or put a form on your website. Then you can contact these people each month with details of your latest products, services and promotions. Another profitable business system.

Workbook:

In the appropriate place in your From Imagination to Implementation *Workbook, fill in the funnel for your business. Start at the top with a cheap or free product you can use to attract people and end with your most expensive product. The price must go up with each step and each step must push people down the funnel. If there are steps you can't fill in with your existing offerings, think of something new that you could add to your business to fill the gap.*

Upselling

'Would you like fries with that?' This is, without doubt, the most well-known upselling phrase in business. I don't even need to tell you where it's from. Upselling is an extremely simple yet effective way to increase profits. How much does it cost McDonald's to ask people if they would like fries? It costs precisely nothing. Most of the time the response is, 'No thanks', or, 'If I

197

wanted the damn fries I would have asked for them in the first place, so just give me my burger you annoying little brat'. And McDonald's is well aware of this. But all it needs is one customer in ten, or one in 20, to say: 'Why yes, thank you very much. I hadn't considered having fries with my meal. What a wonderful suggestion!' This gives McDonald's, over time, a noticeable profit increase for virtually zero effort.

Upselling is the concept of encouraging people to spend more money than they had originally planned to, either by pushing them up to the next model in the range or suggesting something extra that they could buy. It happens at the point of sale (as opposed to the back-end, which is encouraging people to come back to make further purchases). It's as simple as noticing what a customer is buying and suggesting something else that might be of interest. If somebody is browsing through your computer store and asks you about the merits of a particular machine, you can give her all the details of the one she is interested in, but then also point out the next model up, which is faster, has more memory, and a larger screen for only another $250. Or, if she is set on a particular model, you can upsell her by suggesting disks or extra memory or an extended warranty (a very common upselling item).

Using upselling in your business

Here are some things to consider when using upselling in your business:

¤ To create an 'upsale', pay attention to what a customer is buying, and suggest another item or upgrade that will benefit him or her. So our computer seller can ask, 'Do you have a cable modem?' or 'Do you need a back-up drive?'

¤ As McDonald's understand, the best way to encourage an upsell can be to pose it as a question.

¤ Don't go for the hard sell or you might unsell instead. Customers who are satisfied with what they are about to buy will simply get annoyed at a vigorous attempt to upsell.

¤ Keep in mind when trying to upsell that quite often it won't work. If you achieve a 10 per cent or 15 per cent success rate, you are doing well. This will add nicely to your profits with minimal effort. Upselling provides you with bonus sales—you are not trying to make it the main source of income for your business.

¤ If somebody is buying a $175 coffee table, you're not going to be able to upsell her to a $7000 lounge suite. Have a range of lower priced items in your range that will be useful for upselling and will be needed by most or all of your buyers. For example, when I worked at The Athlete's Foot and I was helping someone choose a shoe, I often offered a spray that would make the shoes water resistant. Of course, having just paid $180 for nice shoes, people were happy to pay another $12 to look after them. Always upsell to a cheaper item. What can you add to your business?

A great way to upsell people at the point of purchase (in store) is to offer them a free checklist that is aimed at educating and helping customers with whatever they have purchased. For example, a paint store can offer customers a guide called 'How to ensure a breathtaking paint job', which is basically a checklist of all the things needed to create a breathtaking paint job, such as rollers, drop sheets, a little brush for edges—you get the idea. This is seen by customers as a helpful guide because it includes tips and techniques. It's amazing how many extra purchases people make based on such a checklist. It's a passive upsell.

Warranties are another great upsell example. In electrical stores, for instance, items often come with a one- or two-year warranty. Many stores offer an upgrade—say, to four years. This may only cost $100, so many people will take it up. I know I've done so, many times. But here's where the stores really make money—I've never used it!

Another great example is the many additions you can get with your car when you make a purchase from an auto dealer. The air conditioning, power windows, alloy wheels and metallic paint add to the dealer's profit margin.

Cross-selling

Cross-selling is the concept of convincing a current customer who has already purchased one product to purchase other—usually complementary products from another division of the same company. For example, when customers open a cheque or savings account at a bank, the bank sees this as an opportunity to cross-sell other financial services, such as investment advice, mutual funds, credit cards and home loans. It's easy to see how banks use this method. You will often receive a discount on another product if you already bank there—for example, you might have the fees waived on your savings account if you sign up to a home loan. Telecommunications companies also do this. Most of them offer packages where, for example, if you sign up your home phone, internet and mobile with them you receive a discount, bonus calls or extra downloads. Upselling is similar but it is usually more specific to the particular product and adds to the price of the initial product. See if there are any ways you can cross-sell—for example, by creating packages or discounts if people buy a range of your products or services.

Chapter 15

From imagination to...

networking

> Networking is an essential skill for most business people,
> but especially for entrepreneurs.
>
> <about.com>

Key points

¤ Networking may lead to business opportunities and partnerships, and provide exposure for your business.

¤ Networking is not just about meeting people, it's about creating ongoing relationships.

¤ There are many organisations you can join that will provide you with networking opportunities. Take advantage of them!

¤ Prepare an 'elevator speech' so that you are always prepared if you unexpectedly meet somebody who might be interested in your business.

Entrepreneurship can be a lonely journey, especially if you are working from home by yourself. That's why it is important to *network* and create a *team*. Business networking is all about making connections with other people and organisations. It involves establishing mutually beneficial relationships with other businesses and potential customers. This is very important for all entrepreneurs, especially in the early days. The more actively you become involved in the business community, the more you will benefit. Business networking will increase the exposure of your business and generate leads; it can also lead to joint ventures and teamwork.

Creating a team does not mean having business partners or selling equity to others. You can have a team of people in your industry or not, but if you do, this team will give you support, guidance, keep your feet on the ground and simply make the journey more fun. When you are working nine to five for a company, you usually have people around you who provide support. For an entrepreneur often going it alone, a good network provides this. You can join a mastermind group, a referral organisation, a business association or even all three. All of these groups will give you opportunities to meet other businesspeople of varying experience and backgrounds, as well as provide useful products and services. These are discussed later in the chapter.

There are many ways you can network and create a team:

¤   Attend networking dinners, meetings or functions that are designed just for this purpose.

¤   Attend corporate events.

¤   Have a stand at a trade show (share a stand if cost is a problem).

¤   Join a business association.

¤   Host a business function or seminar.

¤   Sponsor a charity.

¤   Help out at the local school.

Basically, anything you do that brings you into contact with other people and businesses provides a networking opportunity. A friend of mine is in a basketball team that plays during the day on a weekday—the competition is half about playing and half about meeting other businesspeople. You never know who you might meet. You could bump into a CEO at your golf course or a bank manager at a birthday party.

As a good example of what can happen when you network, here's the story of how I found a publisher for this book. Earlier I mentioned my friend Steve McKnight, who wrote the best-selling *From 0 to 130 Properties in 3.5 Years*. He and I ended up with the same publisher, completely by chance! I had discussed my book idea with a friend, who said he might know somebody who could help me find a publisher. He knew a printer, and

> **Pete's tip: here's my card ...**
>
> *Take your business cards with you everywhere. And don't be shy about offering them to people who show an interest. It's a great way to spread the word about your business. Don't forget to ask for their card as well.*

this printer agreed to make a few inquires about my book idea. I didn't think much more about it after the initial conversation with my friend, but a few weeks later I received a call from a publisher who was interested in my idea. It was the same person who had published Steve's book!

Networking and creating a team will help you build your business in many ways:

¤ Meeting others in your industry will help you keep up with what's going on and what the current issues are.

¤ You will raise the profile of your business as more people get to know you.

¤ You may meet some people you can form a joint venture with (more on this in chapter 16).

¤ You can share ideas with other entrepreneurs. We all know the power of the forest from the trees analogy.

¤ And most importantly, you may get leads for some work. For example, if you design websites, maybe the person sitting next to you at the conference is looking for somebody to design her site.

Pete's tip: didn't we meet at...?

Networking is not just about meeting people, it's about making a connection with them. It doesn't matter how many people you meet if they all forget you five minutes later. Engage with people and tell them about your business.

While networking, you will most likely come into contact with the competition. This is not a bad thing. Meeting others in your field can be a good chance to discuss the issues relevant to your industry. Of course, you're not going to discuss the recipe for your secret sauce but you can discuss broader issues. For example, maybe there is new legislation on the horizon that will affect your industry or maybe you are both having problems with the same supplier. Talking about such issues will benefit both businesses without giving away any secret corporate information.

Creating 'network' and 'team' opportunities

There are organisations that provide great business networks. Just type 'business networking' into a search engine to see the many options available. Some organisations are specifically created to provide networking opportunities, others have a more general business focus but are still very useful for meeting people.

Let's consider three options:

¤ Mastermind groups—for example, the Paragon Club. These types of groups are designed to act as a support group and/or 'board of directors'.

¤ Referral groups—for example, BNI (Business Network International) is designed purely to provide leads.

¤ Business associations—for example, the Melbourne Junior Chamber of Commerce, CPA Australia and young lawyers associations provide networking, education and guidance.

I strongly suggest you join one or two of these types of groups, or all three if you can. I am a member of BNI, the Melbourne Junior Chamber of Commerce and the Paragon Club, and all three have been an invaluable resource and provided great support.

Let's have a look at each type of organisation.

Mastermind groups

The term 'mastermind' was coined by Napoleon Hill (author of *Think and Grow Rich*). He defined the principle as the 'coordination of knowledge and effort of two or more people, who work toward a definite purpose, in the spirit of harmony'.

A business mastermind group is a collection of people who get together—perhaps fortnightly or monthly—to offer mutual support, advice and encouragement. It provides a 'board of directors' for people who work for themselves or in a very small organisation. You will be able to bounce ideas off other people before putting them into action, discuss problems you are having and share your experiences with the group. You can gain valuable feedback from people who have been in business longer than you have, or who work in a different industry and therefore might have other ideas about how to approach a problem. Being part of such a group is a great way to get practical support for your business venture.

A mastermind group also provides motivation, as you will be held accountable at each meeting. If you have a great idea at one meeting and don't follow through, the other members of the group will want to know why.

As part of a mastermind group you will learn how to systematically assess a business idea, improve your decision making and contribute to the success of a team. You may also hear expert speakers on various topics, present yourself and your business to the group, review presentations from other members, participate in discussions and work on a range of projects together. This all occurs in a friendly, supportive environment. The aim is to be constructive, not critical, and to help people fill the gaps in their knowledge and experience. It's also a fantastic way to develop business relationships.

For me, masterminding stands out as the single pivotal principle with which anyone can dominate their market in a very short period of time.

Jay Abraham — marketing expert and author

There are business mastermind groups that you can join or you can start one yourself. I'm a member of the Paragon Club <www.paragonclub.com.au>, one of the pre-eminent commercial mastermind groups in Australia. The Paragon Club offers 12-session programs. The sessions run once a month and consist of face-to-face business coaching. There are also other meetings, special events and international study tours available to members, at an extra cost.

People are required to go through an application process to be accepted into the Paragon Club. It is aimed at talented and high-achieving individuals who have something to offer. So if you are interested, make sure you put together a good application, because acceptance is not automatic. Present yourself and your business as strongly as you can and outline what your goals are. You will have to sell yourself, but this is a good thing because it means that if you get in you are working with other very talented and highly motivated individuals.

I've found the Paragon Club to be an invaluable support. It's a great way to meet other enthusiastic businesspeople. You will receive great encouragement, and having a group of people to bounce ideas off is fantastic if you usually work alone. The Paragon Club operates in Melbourne and, at the time of writing, it is starting up in other states.

Referral groups

The aim of a referral group is to generate leads for your business. Each group operates slightly differently, but they generally involve regular meetings (usually fortnightly or monthly) where group members have an opportunity to present themselves and their business to other members. Each member of the group then becomes part of your 'sales force', and will refer any work to you if the opportunity arises and you will do the same for them.

These meetings are very productive. People attend specifically to make contacts, so it's a great way to generate work and also find businesses that can help you. It's all about word-of-mouth marketing. Members usually have references checked, so you can be confident in the people you are referring. You may also gain access to books and audio programs, be able to attend other meetings and functions, receive a newsletter, be listed in a trade directory and have opportunities to attend workshops.

A referral company will often operate in small groups in different locations. You may have a group near you. For obvious reasons, usually only one person from a professional category is allowed to join a group — for example, if you are a website designer and your local group already has a website designer as a member, you will have to find a group in another location.

I am a member of the referral group BNI <www.bni.com.au>, which operates in chapters located all around Australia (and the world). If you sign up, the other BNI members in your chapter will carry your business cards with them and recommend you to other businesses that may be able to use your services (and of course you do the same). You can find your nearest chapter on BNI's website, along with a list of upcoming events.

Being a member of BNI is like having a team of salespeople working for you. I have seen people experience great success using BNI and I have also made some great contacts this way. BNI has helped a lot with On Hold Advertising. Through it, I found plenty of people who were interested in On Hold's services and also created some good business relationships. You can sign up for 12 or 24 months and while there is a fee it's a very good investment for your business. If you are interested, you can attend a meeting to see how it works before signing up.

If you don't act now while it's fresh in your mind, it will probably join the list of things you were always going to do but never quite got around to. Chances are you'll also miss some opportunities.

Paul Clitheroe

Business associations

There are many different types of business associations that you can join. Whatever your industry, there is probably a relevant organisation. Some examples are CPA Australia (Certified Practising Accountants), the Young Lawyers Association, the Professional Photographers Association of Australia, the Australian Nursing Federation, the Australian Association of Automotive Electricians and the Australian Publishers Association. There are also state- and city-based chambers of commerce and junior chambers of commerce.

Such organisations can offer:

¤   education, such as workshops and seminars

¤   training

¤   conferences

¤   industry news and information

¤   industry statistics

¤   online resources

¤   newsletters and other publications

¤   advice

¤   information on rates

¤   social functions

¤   industry awards.

The list is almost endless.

These groups provide great opportunities to meet other people and develop relationships, and you will benefit from the many services that they offer. Find out what organisations are available for your industry and also what general business groups you can join.

I am a member of the Melbourne Junior Chamber of Commerce MJCC, <www.mjcc.org.au>, which is a not-for-profit organisation that represents Melbourne businesspeople under the age of 40. The aim of the MJCC is to provide 'young businesspeople with personal and leadership opportunities through professional business training, social interaction and practical involvement in project management'. There are various levels of membership, with fees starting at under $100. You can sign up to the MJCC's free email list without becoming a member and there are also useful links on its website.

There are other similar organisations around Australia, such as the Sydney Junior Chamber of Commerce and the Brisbane Junior Chamber of Commerce. See if there is a junior chamber of commerce available in your city.

Going up?

You should be ready to network at any time, not just in a business environment. Meeting people at a party, on the golf course, out with friends—you never know when you may meet somebody with whom you could create a useful business relationship. This is why you should have what is referred to as an 'elevator speech' ready to go. When you get chatting to somebody in a lift on the way to the top floor, or anywhere for that matter, you'll be able to give him or her a brief but informative spiel about who you are and what you do.

> Pete's tip: it's not what you know...
>
> *It's not what you know or who you know—it's who knows you.*

You should take time to prepare your elevator speech. You don't necessarily have to write a speech as such, but you should know exactly what you will say to somebody if you have 12 floors to present your business. To get started, have a think about your USP. If you had to sum up your business in 15 words, what would you say? If you had to sum up your best product or service in 20 words, what would you say? Prepare a list of the five most important features of your business and summarise these.

For every sale you miss because you're too enthusiastic, you will miss a hundred because you're not enthusiastic enough.
Zig Ziglar — motivational speaker and author

If you have just 30 seconds to make an impression on somebody, you don't want to present a confused rambling about your business because you hadn't thought about it beforehand. Be prepared to sell people on your idea in 30 seconds. You never know—they might turn into a customer or a joint venture partner. Of course this won't happen in the lift, but you are hoping to create enough interest in a short space of time that the conversation ends with an exchange of business cards and then a follow-up.

Structuring your elevator speech

Instead of just telling people what you do, use the 'You know how…' approach to engage them and show them how you can solve a problem. For example, I could tell people what On Hold Advertising does by simply saying, 'We create on-hold advertising messages for businesses'. But the most likely response to this will simply be, 'Okay…' It's not a good way to get the message across.

Let's try a different approach. When somebody asks you what you do, try saying, 'You know how…' This should illicit a 'yes' from the person you are speaking with. Then you continue, 'Well, what we do is…'

For On Hold Advertising, it goes like this:

'You know how annoying it is when you get put on hold and are subjected to chimes, loud radio or—worse still—silence?'

I wait for the other person to say *yes*.

'Well, what we do at On Hold Advertising is ensure this doesn't happen to your callers by getting inside your business and creating

Pete's tip: practise

Practise your elevator speech on your family, friends or colleagues. Have them ask you questions, so that you can prepare yourself for what people might ask. Or you could go to a large hotel and ride up and down in the lift…

a tailored money-making on-hold marketing message as unique as your business, which will turn your callers into customers. We even insist on a free trial and ensure you are happy in order to make the decision a no-brainer.'

How's that? Much more interesting for the other person and you've shown how you can solve a problem that he or she might not even have thought about. Think about how you can apply this approach to your business. The key is not simply telling people what you do but showing them how you solve problems.

As with your marketing, you're not aiming for 100 per cent success. If you give your elevator speech to 10 people in a week and you hear back

Workbook:

On the elevator speech page of your From Imagination to Implementation Workbook, *write down the five most important things that you would like to communicate about your business in a short space of time. Anticipate five questions that might result from this spiel and prepare your answers.*

from three of them, you have done well. That's three contacts you may not have made if you had fumbled your way through the conversation.

Chapter 16

From imagination to...

team force

> Coming together is a beginning. Keeping together is progress.
> Working together is success.
>
> **Henry Ford**

Key points

¤ Teaming up with other organisations can increase your exposure, lower your costs and provide access to more customers.

¤ Teaming up means you can offer added value to your clients.

¤ Check out a business very carefully before you team up with it.

A great way to boost your business is to enlist the help of others; again it's all about leverage, and getting the most out of what you have and have in reach. This can be in the form of joint ventures, affiliate programs, referrals, cross promotions—just about any way you can think of to join up with other organisations, whether they are in your field or not. This will give you more exposure and access to new ponds (markets). Be creative and see what ways you can come up with to create a team force.

The E.J. Whitten Foundation and selling the 'G

I initially became involved with the E.J. Whitten Foundation because I wanted to donate some of my profits to charity—nothing more, nothing less. I chose this foundation because of the obvious link with what I was doing—Ted Whitten was a football great. At first, I donated 10 per cent from each sale but this later developed into a partnership. For this joint venture I created a select series of frames that included a photo of Teddy's final lap of the MCG (which has been voted the most memorable moment in the history of the MCG), which we marketed and sold through the E.J. Whitten Foundation network of supporters and associates. This strategic alliance was a winner for all involved as it generated a significant amount of money for both myself and the foundation, along with keeping awareness of the venture and the foundation in the marketplace. The key to a successful partnership is that both parties benefit, and in teaming up with me to create the E.J. frames, the foundation benefited because the more sales I made the more money it received to use to fight cancer.

Teaming up with the E.J. Whitten Foundation opened up opportunities for me that otherwise probably wouldn't have happened. For example, I received exposure through *The Footy Show* and the E.J. Whitten Legends game, which was shown on Channel 9, and I was involved with Brownlow Medal events and grand final lunches. I was able to do this because the E.J. Whitten Foundation is still involved in football and my alliance with it opened those doors for me. And once again, the more exposure I received, the more I sold and the more I donated, so the foundation was more than happy to be involved in this way. It was helping itself by helping me.

I also created a special one-off Ted Whitten frame, which was featured on Channel 9 during the E.J. Whitten Legends game, and we also had articles appear in the *Herald Sun* featuring Ted Whitten Jnr holding one of the special frames. People were directed to my site, where I was running an online auction for the frame as a fundraiser. This generated a great deal of interest and sent lots of traffic to my site.

As I said earlier, I'm a great believer in karma. If you create an alliance with a charity motivated only by your own business needs, it will come back to haunt you somewhere down the line. But if you are genuinely interested in helping others, your business and the charity will both benefit.

The E.J. Whitten Foundation

The E.J. Whitten Foundation is dedicated to increasing awareness of prostate cancer and raising money for research into the disease. Ted Whitten died from prostate cancer in 1995. If you would like more information, or to make a donation, go to <www.ejwhittenfoundation.com.au>.

Creating alliances

Every business can create strategic alliances to improve sales via referrals and economies of scale in marketing. For example:

¤ Footwear retailers and podiatrists—they can share mailing list details and conduct a mail-out together. This reduces the cost and increases the number of people reached.

¤ Clothing stores and image consultants—the store and the consultant can provide customers with a 5 per cent discount when they go from one to the other.

¤ Landscapers and home painters—if you are a landscaper, team up with a painter and give each others' cards or brochures to clients when you finish a job.

> I prefer to think of joint ventures in terms of what I call a host-beneficiary relationship. In essence, you serve as a 'host' introducing someone else's complementary and appropriate products or services to your customers ...
> **Jay Abraham — marketing expert and author**

Strategic alliances are created simply by approaching the business you want to work with. Give the business owner a call and explain what you have in mind or prepare a formal proposal and arrange a meeting with him or her. Most importantly, make sure you can clearly explain what is in it for the other business. You can't simply ring up another business and say, 'Hey, can I use your mailing list?' Clearly explain what you are asking and what you are offering in return. If you come up with an idea that benefits both businesses, you will have a good chance of your proposal being accepted.

Marketing author and expert Jay Abraham calls joint ventures a 'host–beneficiary' relationship and you can benefit on either side. Be a host and introduce your clients to other people's products and you will add some sales commission to your profits. Be a beneficiary and you will get more sales in and expand your market for the cost of the commissions given to the host.

Let's have a look at some of the ways you can create strategic alliances in your business.

Referrals

Having a referral agreement with another business is perhaps the easiest way to create teamwork—you simply refer business to each other. For example, The Athlete's Foot stores have implemented a very successful referral system with podiatrists across the country. Podiatrists often refer patients to Athlete's Foot stores to purchase quality footwear, as they know the staff are heavily trained in making sure the shoe chosen actually 'fits' for better comfort and support. The Athlete's Foot stores often refer customers who have great 'needs' to the podiatrists they have a relationship with. It's a perfect win-win relationship that also benefits the clients.

There is no profit sharing or joint operation—the benefit to both businesses is that they receive the business as a result of the referral. Such a referral system also means that you are providing added value to your clients. They don't have to shop around to find the other products or services they need and if they have had a good experience with you they will have confidence that the business you are sending them to will also provide good service.

You can provide referrals in a number of ways:

¤ You can simply suggest the other business to your client. If you can, give him or her a name of somebody to speak to.

¤ You can encourage referrals by agreeing on a bonus with your referral partner—for example, 'If you go to Fred's Printing, you'll get a 5 per cent discount if you say that I sent you'. You could even create vouchers for this.

¤ Provide a link on your website to the business's website. Make sure this is recognisable as a referral, not just a link—for example, 'We recommend ACME Removal Services because their removalists won't break your stuff'. Okay, perhaps something a bit better than that, but you get the idea!

¤ Provide business cards, brochures or referral pads to the other business, to hand out to customers. For example, a while ago I went to see my dentist and she recommended a particular type of mouthwash. She pulled out a pad that had various Colgate products listed on it and ticked the one she wanted me to use. I simply went to the chemist and handed the piece of paper to the pharmacist and she gave me the Colgate product. What an easy sale for Colgate!

Another great way to use referrals is to conduct a mail-out to your customers recommending the products or services of your partner, and your partner does the same by recommending your offerings. You don't need to get further involved, you simply direct your clients to the other business and the other business pays you a commission on each sale. You can write a sales letter outlining the product or service, why you think it will be useful for your customer and why you recommend it. This is another great reason to have a customer database—you can use it to generate commission income.

Joint ventures

A joint venture is where you team up with another organisation for a particular project (as opposed to an ongoing commitment, which is a partnership). For example, if you are releasing a new line of computers you could team up with a software provider to create a promotional package. Both you and the software company promote the package in your own businesses and the profits can be split according to whatever agreement you reach. You can also create a new product or service through a joint venture. For example, if you are a landscape gardener, you could form a venture with a home renovator to offer complete house makeover packages.

Joint ventures give both organisations access to more customers, provide greater sales and more distribution channels, and bring a wider range of knowledge and skills to the operation. They can also reduce costs because resources and expenses can be shared—for example, you can share the cost of a mail-out or a telemarketing campaign, or the costs of distribution.

Another great advantage of a joint venture is that you double your resources. When you are just getting started, perhaps you can start a joint venture with a business that has been going for years and you can leverage its experience. Or you can team up with a business in a completely different field to use their skills.

Here are some other ideas for joint ventures:

¤ If you are an ideas person but you're not too good with the technical side, team up with an engineer to see what new products you can create.

¤ Team up with a company that distributes overseas. You can expand your distribution overseas without setting it up yourself and the other business gets another product to offer to its customers.

¤ Open up a stand inside a large store and give the store a percentage of the profits.

¤ If you don't know where the commas go, have somebody write your manuals for you. Sell the manuals on your website and split the profits 50–50.

¤ Share office space with somebody in the same industry, and share customers and ideas.

If another business is a leader in your area, take advantage of this and get involved. Remember, though, that you must always offer something in return, which creates symbiosis.

There are many examples of symbiotic relationships in nature. For example, gobies sometimes form symbiotic relationships with other species, such as shrimps. A shrimp will create a burrow in the sand and the shrimp and the goby will live in this. The shrimp has poorer eyesight than the goby, and if the goby senses danger and swims into the burrow, the shrimp will follow. The goby gets a place to live and shelter and the shrimp gets an air-raid siren. Symbiosis! There are also many examples of large fish that have smaller fish swimming around with them to help keep the larger fish clean. The large fish gets a maid, the smaller fish gets protection.

> **Pete's tip: create symbiotic relationships**
>
> *I sometimes refer to teaming up as being a symbiotic relationship. If another business has been operating for years and has a huge customer base, create a symbiotic relationship with this organisation. Don't let being small stop you.*

Keep this in mind when seeking business partnerships. You must offer something and if you are small you can still offer something useful to a large organisation.

Sharing customer databases

Sharing customer details with another business in your field (that is not a direct competitor) is a great way for you to both increase your customer lists. You can do this in a number of ways:

- You can simply exchange customer lists so you can both do individual marketing.

- You can conduct a mail-out together to both lists.

- You can telemarket to both lists.

- If the other company doesn't want your list, you can ask to use its list and offer it 10 per cent of all sales that you achieve using the details it provides.

Make sure that the customers on *both* lists are aware that their details may be passed on. You've probably seen the option on some forms that states, 'Tick here to allow us to pass on your details to other companies that have products or services that may interest you'. Make sure you include this, otherwise you'll have plenty of angry customers. Privacy is very important. You can't pass on customer details without their knowledge. Interested customers will be happy to tick this box because they will want to receive the information.

In this new wave of technology, you can't do it all yourself, you have to form alliances.
Carlos Slim Helu — businessman and the richest man in Mexico

Affiliate programs

I call affiliate programs 'franchising lite'. An affiliate program is where you promote somebody else's website (usually through a link on your own site) but you are not part of its business or marketing structure. Your business can be on either end of an affiliate program—you can enlist people to promote your business and pay a commission, or you can promote other businesses and receive a commission for each lead you generate.

Amazon used this approach to help build its business. Amazon encourages people to place on their own website links to books for sale on Amazon. If a customer clicks on this link and buys a book, the website owner receives a commission. Amazon seems to be doing quite well.

Affiliate programs are a great way to attract people to your site and to spread the word about your business. There are affiliate networks that you can sign up to and you can also create your own affiliate program on your site (though this can be more complicated and time consuming). For a relatively low cost you can attract customers you may otherwise not have reached. This can also be a great way to create an automated system that generates profits for little effort.

If you would like to sign up to my affiliate program, go to: <www.preneurmarketing.com.au/affiliate.php>

Cross promotion

Here are some other simple suggestions that will help you and your partner promote each others' businesses:

- Include a flyer for the other business when you send out an invoice.

- Put its business cards on your counter or in your office.

- Put up a poster for the other business in your store.

- Mention the other business in your sales letters.

- Share an ad in the local newspaper.

- If your partner's business is seasonal, promote its business during its slow times.

- Host a publicity event together

- Conduct a radio interview together.

Your partner will, of course, do the same for you.

The possibilities are endless. See what you can come up with that will make both of your businesses stand out.

Win-win-win

The essence of any type of business teamwork is that both sides benefit. This can be through reaching new customers, reducing costs, increased visibility in the marketplace—anything that will ultimately result in more profits. Whatever you expect to receive from another business, you must be willing to offer the same in return. Both businesses must win.

If you wish to team up with another organisation but it's not interested in working with you, try offering a financial incentive. For example, if you are just starting out and wish to open a booth in a large store, you may not have anything to offer in return because you are still small. But if the store lets you open a booth, you can give it 15 per cent of all profits made from the booth. I'm sure it'll be interested in that!

The third win is that your customers benefit as well. You will be offering them more products or services that they are interested in, referring them to other businesses that are good at what they do and possibly giving them cheaper prices along the way.

> Great teamwork is the only way we create the breakthroughs that define our careers.
> **Pat Riley — 2006 NBA champion basketball coach**

Choose carefully

You must fully check out any businesses that you choose to team up with. I cannot emphasise this point enough. If you align yourself with another organisation in any way, its problems reflect on you. If you refer a customer to another business that does a poor job, this reflects badly on you, and you will lose a customer and damage the reputation of your business.

Pete's tip: write it down

Whatever type of team force you come up with, make sure you have a written agreement with the other business. Just include all the elements of the relationship and who is to do what.

Check out a business or organisation carefully before you team up. Buy its products and use its services. Surf the net to find out about them. Talk to the managers. Get as much information as you can. Only when you are confident that teaming up with this business will reflect positively on you and your business should you go ahead.

Chapter 17

From imagination to...

barter profits

> Become a student of change. It is the only thing that will remain constant.
>
> **Anthony J D'Angelo**

Key points

¤ Barter will open you up to a whole new economic system, allowing you to reach customers that prefer to trade this way.

¤ Barter is a great way to fill up your down time or offload excess stock.

¤ Barter frees up cash flow and leverages your business.

¤ Used wisely, barter will increase your profits!

Bartering is a method of trade that is conducted through the exchange of goods or services rather than money. It is one of the oldest forms of trade in existence—it's been around since people had anything to barter with. Over the centuries people have bartered cows, grain, food, jewellery, alcohol and just about anything else of value. During the Middle Ages Europeans travelled the world, trading furs and other items for silk and spices. Barter has also seen a resurgence during tough times when cash has been scarce—for example, during the Great Depression.

Today, barter is used by big businesses that are willing to be creative. One of the great barter stories of recent times is how Pepsi became the number one cola in Russia. Instead of buying the Pepsi with cash, Russia granted Pepsi the North American distribution rights to Stolichnaya Vodka. Russia essentially paid for the Pepsi with vodka, which Pepsi then sold—with great success—in America. Pepsi made a fortune in both markets!

Another great modern example of bartering is the babysitting clubs. This concept involves a group of parents getting together to form a group and paying for babysitting in tokens, which are then used to pay for someone in the group to care for your little one while you have a well-deserved break. No money changes hands, just your time. Usually the club will nominate a person to keep the records.

When I discovered the world of barter, it was much like the first time I went scuba diving. An entire world existed within my own world and I wasn't aware of it.
Jay Conrad Levinson — *Guerrilla Marketing*

Any business can barter its goods or services. For example, if you are looking at opening a florist you could approach a local restaurant and offer to supply it with fresh table flowers each week, in exchange for a $100 meal every Sunday. The cost to supply $100 worth of flowers to the restaurant would not actually be $100—maybe the wholesale price is only $30. Thus, as the restaurant's florist you get to eat out each week, have a $100 meal and only be $30 out of pocket; effectively you have saved $70.

Trade exchanges

Today there are organised, third-party record keepers called trade exchanges, which have thousands of members in almost every industry that help facilitate these types of contra transactions. It's a small but rapidly expanding segment of the economy. The member directories of these exchanges are the size of a large *Yellow Pages* and they have members all over the world. The exchange acts as a conduit in the transaction. It's like a bank, and a lot of people lose sight of this fact.

To explain how this works let's use a typical example again; let's say you are a florist and that you wish to get some printing done for your business to attract extra sales. In the 'cash economy' the printer may charge $10000 for the flyers, brochures and business cards that you need. If you approached the printer to try to work out a direct contra (like the one with the restaurant above), it's fairly unlikely the transaction would occur as the printer would have no use for, say, 1000 $10 bunches of flowers to cover the $10000 printing cost.

However, a trade exchange makes this contra deal possible, as exchanges offer members an interest-free line of credit to initiate and support trading. If the florist and the printer are members of the same trade exchange, the florist can use its *interest free* line of credit to pay for the $10000 worth of printing, in what are referred to as trade dollars (T$). Instead of being in debt or owing the printer directly, the florist now owes the 'exchange' T$10000. To pay off this T$10000 debt, the florist over the next 12 months might sell T$2000 worth of roses to the printer, T$500 worth to an accountant, T$6000 to a reception centre and so on, all of whom are members of the trade exchange. So you can now see how this contra transaction could work and be facilitated using an exchange.

Basically you are going to get the greatest benefit from your trade exchange if you use it only in your down time or when you have excess stock — it's not designed to replace cash business, just complement it. There are a few costs involved (which are explained later in this chapter), but basically during your quieter periods you can offer your products or services for 'barter dollars', which you keep in your bank until you have the need for a product or service offered by a memeber of the exchange.

Let's look at it from a dollars and cents perspective. For a florist to sell 1000 T$10 bunches of flowers and pay off the T$10000 debt, it would obviously incur out-of-pocket costs to purchase the flowers at wholesale. I am not a florist, but for this example let's use the same costs as above and say the average wholesale cost of a bunch of flowers (which the florist sells for $10) is $3. The florist will incur a total 'cash' cost of $3000 to supply 1000 bunches to the exchange members.

Being a member of a trade exchange is not free. There are fees involved for the exchange to act as the record keeper. These fees are explained later, but for the sake of making this example easier let's say the fees for selling T$10 000 worth of flowers are $1000 in cash. Therefore the total cash cost to the florist to pay back the T$10 000 in flowers is only $4000 ($3000 for the flowers and $1000 in fees)—that's a $6000 *cash saving!*

In other words, at the end of the day the florist has received $10 000 worth of printing for the cost of $4000. The florist is only having to pay 40 cents in the dollar for every purchase it makes using the trade exchange—now that's power! But it gets better. These 1000 bunches of flowers are generally going to be sales the florist would not have otherwise made. That's new business to the florist and it has saved the 1000 bunches it may have had to otherwise throw out and write off.

Looking at it from the printer's point of view, it has received $10 000 worth of new business it would have otherwise had to forfeit. The printer is free to spend these trade dollars on accounting services, holidays, phone bills, graphic design and whatever else it needs, which it would have otherwise had to pay cash for. And from its perspective, to provide the T$10 000 in printing the printer may only have had raw costs of $4500.

Pete's tip: tax

Worried about the tax implications of barter? It's easy—one trade dollar equals one cash dollar and you claim income and expenses in the normal way. Easy!

What about overheads and wages, you may be asking— they were not included in the calculations. *Exactly right!* As the idea for activity in a trade exchange is to bring in new sales and/or take up down time or idle stock, there are going to be no extra overheads to provide the additional services. It's only the incremental costs that need to be considered. The rent is already being covered by your cash customers, as are the wages, electricity and all of the other overheads. A trade exchange is designed to help milk every spare moment of down time (printer) or idle inventory (florist).

Cost of trade dollars

The raw cost is your cost of trade dollars—that's what it costs you in cash to sell an item on trade and pay back a trade dollar spent. There are two elements that make up a 'cost of trade'—the raw costs to supply or replace the product you have sold, and the fees payable to the exchange for facilitating and recording the transaction.

In most exchanges the fees are broken up into two parts—fees for when you sell a product to an exchange member and fees for when you purchase from a member of the exchange. These average about 5 per cent on both sides of the transaction. Yes, a little more than the typical 1 per cent to 3 per cent charged by the banks for transacting a Visa payment *but* do the banks proactively bring you new business or act as your purchasing agent and help you put your money back into your business? (This is explained in the example provided.)

The calculation to work out the cost of your trade dollar is:

Florist:

Sale price for a bunch of flowers	$10
Cost of flowers from wholesaler	$3
Fees to the trade exchange (approx. 10 per cent)	$1
Total costs to supply the flowers	$4
Cost of T$ (costs/sale)	40 per cent or 40¢ in the dollar

For $4 cash you now have access to $10 worth of trade dollars. So when the florist goes and spends $10 in the trade exchange it only costs $4 in cash—that's a $6 saving.

Service industry professionals—such as accountants, lawyers and writers—would only take on work from a trade exchange member if they had idle time, which would otherwise not be billable, thus they don't factor in the cost of time.

Accountant:

Sale price of item	$50 per hour
Raw replacement cost	$8 in paper
Fees (approx. 10 per cent)	$5
Total costs	$13
Cost of T$ (costs/sale)	26 per cent or 26¢ in the dollar

An accountant can use the trade dollars earned to purchase printing, graphic design, advertising in magazines, customer loyalty—whatever they can find in the trade exchange.

Restaurant:

Sale price of item	$60 per meal
Raw replacement cost	$9 in meat, veg and juice
Fees (approx. 10 per cent)	$6
(the staff are already there and being paid for)	$0
Total costs	$17
Cost of T$ (costs/sale)	28 per cent or 28¢ in the dollar

Some nights a restaurant won't be full, but the owner still has to pay the rent, electricity, wages and other costs. The restaurant can use its trade dollars to purchase wine for the restaurant, get the menus printed and offer staff bonuses.

Hotel:

Sale price of item	$120 per night
Raw replacement cost	$6 in laundry and little soaps

Hotel cont'd:

Fees (approx 10 per cent)	$12
Total costs	$18
Cost of T$ (costs/sale)	15 per cent or 15¢ in the dollar

The hotel can use its trade dollars to advertise, develop its website or offer guests restaurant vouchers.

> Never be frightened to take a profit. Better in your pocket then theirs.
> **Michael Levy**

With most trade exchanges there is also a joining fee. To put this start-up cost into perspective, remember in chapter 9 when we spoke about the costs involved in registering your business? These are costs you incur in order to be 'allowed' access to the cash economy in business. Therefore, it would be expected that there would be a cost involved in getting access to the trade economy, right? You are opening your business up to a completely new segment of the economy, so you should consider the costs involved as an investment in your business.

Leverage using trade exchanges

Earlier I mentioned that trade exchanges can help you make additional sales and assist in purchasing. They do this by providing trade brokers whose role it is to assist and support your trading by advertising your goods and services to other members of the exchange, and also by acting as your purchasing agent in sourcing products and services for you to purchase. This is where the difference between Visa fees and trade fees goes, in employing a vast network of trade brokers throughout the country who are acting as your sales department and purchasing officers. If you think that paying an extra 2 per cent to 3 per cent per transaction to have an outsourced team supporting you and doing a fair bit of the work is excessive, you will not last long in business! Remember, it's all about *systems* and *leverage*.

On top of the financial advantages, these other benefits make the fees negligible:

¤ greater exposure for your business

¤ attract business that you otherwise wouldn't have

¤ ability to increase your customer base, which can be leveraged for testimonials and referrals

¤ access to an interest-free line of credit, which can help your cash flow

¤ access to an online auction site similar to eBay but using trade dollars.

Mirror economy

Just like the florist's stock, trade exchanges are not all roses (like that pun?), you will have to work. Similar to the internet, a trade exchange is a business tool—it's not a solution or autonomous affair.

If you can grasp this lesson, and I mean really grasp it, a trade exchange will be one of the most powerful tools in your arsenal. But if you are close-minded it will not work for you. As a side note, did you recognise I said it would not work for you, *not* your industry? Any industry can receive substantial benefits from being involved in a trade exchange but the owner of the business must be open-minded and entrepreneurial. I often hear comments like, 'That wouldn't work for my business/industry'. Well, I say it can and does work for your industry but it will not necessarily work for *you*! There are businesses in literally every industry and of every size. If an ASX-listed company can benefit from a trade exchange, there is absolutely no excuse why you can't.

Whether you think you can or think you can't, either way you are right.
Anonymous

A term I have coined for trade exchanges is 'mirror economy'. I use that term to illustrate how a trade exchange is an economy that works as a mirror to the typical cash economy, in terms of how much effort you have to exert.

For example, in the 'cash economy' if you wanted to get $10 000 worth of printing done and you treat this transaction in isolation, it might look something like this:

1 Spend six sporadic hours (in design and implementation of advertising and sales meetings) to generate $10 000 in gross profit to cover the cost of the printing.

2 Two hours supplying the service or goods to the customers.

3 One hour actually finding an adequate printer and placing the order.

In total, you have spent nine hours to get $10 000 worth of brochures.

Now, trade exchanges work in an opposite (mirror) fashion, in that you will most likely:

1 Spend one hour finding the business.

2 Two hours supplying the service or goods (this obviously doesn't change).

3 Six hours finding the printer to do the work.

> **Pete's tip: finding an exchange**
> *To find one of the many barter exchanges available in Australia, simply type 'trade exchange' or 'barter exchange' into a search engine.*

In total, you have still spent nine hours achieving the end result but the process is reversed (a mirror). Now, with the use of the trade brokers the six hours is an exaggeration, but the point is the harder part of the equation or where you will spend the majority of your time, is in spending the trade dollars. This is because not every business is involved in a trade exchange, so you can't simply walk out your door, turn right and spend trade dollars on the things you want like milk and bread. This doesn't make the exchange wrong or inadequate—I never said that the exchange would be less work time-wise, but it will save you money due to the cost of your trade dollars, as explained above, and this results in more profitable time and more cash in your pocket! *Which is the aim of the game!*

How barter was used in the MCG venture

Here's how I used trade exchange to barter my way to a fatter wallet. The trade exchange I am a member of is Bartercard. Bartercard is the world's largest trade exchange and was actually started in Australia in the early 1990s. It is now used in more than 15 countries and has tens of thousands of members. I first got exposure to Bartercard a few years back when I worked with the Bartercard team in the Geelong Office.

I used this trade exchange to sell a number of the MCG frames to buyers all over the country, which meant I earned thousands of trade dollars I would not have otherwise received. I then used the trade dollars to manufacture the frames. I had the photos for the frames printed in Sydney and shipped directly to me. The plaques were produced in Queensland and the frames were constructed by a fantastic framer in Geelong — again on trade. This meant that all the frames I sold on trade were paid for on trade. The only cash cost I incurred was in the exchange fees.

So if I sold a frame to a Bartercard member for T$495, I had to pay about $50 in cash fees to the trade exchange (the 10 per cent explained above). I then spent T$120 to have the frame produced (plaque, printing and framing), but was left with T$375 trade profit, which I could spend on anything. This profit, spending capacity or 'free money' only really cost me $50 cash — the Bartercard fees. So $50 cash cost resulted in me having T$375 in my barter account that I could spend freely. That's a cost of trade of 13 per cent or 13 cents in the dollar. It gets even better though; instead of just spending that $375 on frivolous things, I used those trade dollars to cover the production costs of the frames I sold for cash. This meant that basically all the income I made from a cash sale was pure profit that I could bank.

I would have been mad not to be involved in a trade exchange for this business. The beauty of it all was that because I started my business at the same time I was involved in the trade exchange, I was able to develop, design and structure my business in a way that maximised my involvement in the trade exchange. This is using systems (chapter 7) to your advantage.

Yes, it took a little more work in finding and coordinating the plaque and photo production from interstate, but for the additional cash profit for every frame I sold it was well worth the effort, plus I didn't do a single thing in promoting the frames—the trade exchange and trade brokers did all the work.

I have also used the trade dollars earned to design and build <www.preneurmarketing.com.au>.

To give you some more examples of how other industries and people I know use trade exchanges, here are a few examples and short stories:

¤ One proactive businessperson I deal with owns a number of car-hire companies around Melbourne. He earns trade dollars renting out cars that would otherwise go unused. Obviously his cost of trade is very low as the cash costs involved in letting someone drive a car are low. He then uses the trade dollars to purchase MCG frames from me, which he donates and directly barters to sporting clubs and charities for sponsorship packages. This way he can use the trade dollars he earns to support charities he believes in and to get sponsorship for cents in the dollar (due to his low cost of trade).

¤ A number of restaurants I know of fill up tables that would otherwise be empty with additional sales on Bartercard. As the restaurant is already open, the wages and overheads are already being covered by the cash-paying clientele. The only direct cost the restraunteurs incur are for the food. They then use the trade dollars earned to purchase their entire wine list.

¤ A pro basketball club sells additional sponsorship packages on trade that it would not have otherwise, which it then uses to pay for the accommodation for the club's away games.

¤ A retail store sells its goods on trade to increase stock turnover, and then uses the trade dollars earned for raffles and bonuses for its VIP customers.

The possibilities of a trade exchange as a tool are infinite and will only be limited by your openness and entrepreneurialism.

Chapter 18

From imagination to...
creative business

> Nothing is impossible to a person who refuses to listen to reason.
>
> **Gary Halbert**

Key points

¤   Be creative!

Pete's random business thoughts...

So what's this chapter all about then? Basically, this is all the good stuff I've collected over the years that didn't fit elsewhere in the book but is too good to leave out. It's a collection of interesting and creative examples, quotes, stories and suggestions that you can learn from. Have a think about each item and how it could apply to your business. Use these as starting points to brainstorm for your business. Hopefully you will generate a few useful ideas. Enjoy!

Advertising isn't everything

A few years ago a business decided to stop spending money on advertising and instead put the advertising money into free shipping for customers. The business world was stunned. How can a business survive like this? But word of mouth created by the free shipping made up for the lack of advertising and the business boomed. Who was it? Amazon.

First Interstate Bank

When Security Pacific Bank merged with Bank of America, many Security Pacific branches were closed. First Interstate Bank rented trucks and parked them outside the branches that were closing, and the First Interstate staff signed up customers as they were leaving.

Your most unhappy customers are your greatest source of learning.
Bill Gates

Dissatisfied customers

In his great book *Free Prize Inside*, Seth Godin—against popular opinion—says that 'people who are happy are your company's worst enemy'. Why? Because 'satisfied customers are unlikely to radically increase your sales'. The most potential for sales growth lies in finding *dissatisfied* people who need your product or service as a solution to their problem.

When you are coming up with a new product or idea, use dissatisfied customers as a barometer, not your current happy customers. If you can satisfy the unhappy campers, then you are on to a good thing. And then of course you have to move on to the next lot.

Disneyland

Have you ever been to Disneyland? When you get off the roller-coaster and other rides, the exit puts you right in the gift shop. A great back-end!

Henry's goal

Henry Ford's primary goal was to make a cheap car, so the Model T was available only in black because this was the cheapest option. He matched his product and his systems to his goal.

But Henry did make a mistake. He concentrated on his goal so much that he didn't create a higher end model and the competition moved in before Henry noticed the opportunity. Perhaps Henry should have had two goals—a low-end model and a high-end model, much as Toyota does with Lexus today.

> Next in importance to having a good aim is to recognize when to pull the trigger.
> **David Letterman**

Idea a day

Remember that what you do with an idea matters just as much as the idea itself. And just to emphasise the fact that ideas are everywhere, there's a great website called Idea a Day <www.idea-a-day.com>. Idea a Day home-delivers your supermarket shopping. No, not really...if you can't figure out what this business does from its title, then I don't think you have what it takes to be an entrepreneur.

My favourite idea from this site is the 'address for life'. Everybody is allocated an address code and then you register your actual delivery address—linked to your code—with the post office. Everybody would have PO box–style privacy and, when you move, you only have to let the post office know and all your mail would be redirected. If anybody wants to get this off the ground, give me a call! I'll be your first customer.

> It's not the idea that matters, it's what you do with it. The real challenge...comes from championing your idea, shepherding it through the system and turning it into reality.
> **Seth Godin**

Risk reversal

Risk reversal is all about removing any 'risk' that the prospect may be feeling and transferring it to your business. For example, I bought an expensive computer recently and I wanted to buy an industrial-strength surge protector to go with it. The one I chose offered a guarantee for up to $70 000 worth of new equipment to replace anything damaged by an electrical surge while connected to their surge protector. So instead of me taking on the risk that this company's product doesn't do what it should, the company itself has taken on the risk.

Marketing expert Jay Abraham is generally credited with creating 'risk reversal', but in fact it was the original marketing guru Claude C Hopkins in his 1923 book *Scientific Advertising* who introduced the concept. He discusses the difference between selling your products and offering a refund for dissatisfied customers, and offering a trial for a week and paying at the end if the product is acceptable. In the second scenario, the risk is transferred from the buyer to the seller. Hopkins gives the example of a man buying a horse. The first salesperson said, 'Take it for a week and if you're not happy I'll refund your money'. The second salesperson said, 'Take the horse for a week, then come and pay me'. The second salesperson got the sale.

To reduce risk for our On Hold Advertising clients, we offer a 60-day free trial. I also offer money back guarantees on all products sold at <preneurmarketing.com.au>.

Google actually relies on our users to help with our marketing. We have a very high percentage of our users who often tell others about our search engine.
Sergey Brin

I'll swap you this paperclip for that house

A Canadian blogger, 26-year-old Kyle MacDonald, started with a red paperclip and an idea, and ended up with a house, just by bartering his way to a slightly increased value with each trade. He has now signed a book publishing deal and sold the movie rights to DreamWorks. He says, 'I was sitting in front of the computer with a paperclip and that is all there was. Now, I am sitting down with some of the biggest producers in Hollywood and the largest publishers in the world'.

The paperclip wars

Speaking of paperclips, in *Free Prize Inside* Godin talks about when paperclips first hit the market and the fierce paperclip marketing battles that ensued. It's true! Godin concludes that there are two ways to separate yourself from the commodity crowd:

- ¤ Build something that nobody else can build (so you can charge more for it). There were many patents filed in an effort to build the better paperclip.

- ¤ Advertise it like crazy to build a brand (so that you can charge enough to make a profit). There was a paperclip advertising battle when the product was first invented.

> Like most businesspeople, I want every aspect of my business to be perfect. I know that this goal is unachievable, but it is nevertheless what I strive to achieve.
> **Bob Parsons — businessman**

Quoting

A friend of mine who runs a painting and tradesperson service requires clients to sign off on the quotes he provides. These quotes include a range of terms and conditions, such as payment terms and penalties if payments are made late. Because he presents the quotes so professionally, not only does it increase the sales presentation, it also lowers the resistance from clients and secures his income. He finds that clients are also more likely to stick to the terms when they have signed their agreement.

> You've got to love what you do to really make things happen.
> **Philip Green — British billionaire businessman**

Negative qualifiers

Make sure in your advertising you also include negative qualifiers. A negative qualifier is something that will actually reduce the amount of calls or clicks you receive—it pre-qualifies the prospects and eliminates the tyre kickers, saving you time and money. The best example of this can be found in Google Adwords campaigns. A lot of people use the internet to search for free information or are price shopping. Including the price of your product or e-book in the ad description may reduce the amount of click-thrus (thus lowering costs) but increase the conversion rate — that is, the percentage of people who click-thru and buy.

Product experience

Make people experience your product. This is obvious for industries such as car sales, but how can you adapt the idea to your product? At the Athlete's Foot store I used to work at we 'plus'd the idea' and actually had a treadmill in store so people who were using the shoes for running could actually go for a short jog and test them out — we all know running is a lot different to walking. And when you call the team at On Hold Advertising, there is a strong chance you will be placed on hold and hear our marketing message. Not only will this help the sales process, it will also reduce returns and customer questions after the sale.

The important thing is not being afraid to take a chance.
Remember, the greatest failure is to not try.
Debbi Fields — founder of Mrs Fields Cookies

Gift vouchers — literally!

Instead of giving a gift 'voucher', why not give customers a gift that is a voucher! If you sell clothes, give away a T-shirt with the offer printed on it. A shoe store could sew the gift certificate onto a sock. A hardware store could engrave small shovels.

Leave a memory

Create an experience for your customers that is from left field, so that it creates a memory for the client. A friend of mine who runs a building company produces a small coffee-table book for clients that has before, during and after photos, along with descriptions. He gives the book to customers when they receive the keys. This is a powerful process as it resonates with clients and keeps the builder fresh in their minds, plus the new homeowners or renovators are so proud that they show this book to all their family and friends.

This is basically a sales tool for my friend's building business. Or you could just do something simple. Drycleaner staff could put mints or handkerchiefs in the breast pocket of suits they clean. When the customer puts his or her suit on a week later, he or she finds a gift from the drycleaner, which reinforces the drycleaner's brand and creates a memorable moment. This will help create word-of-mouth marketing.

Word-of-mouth marketing

An article that was posted on the Customer Evangelists Blog demonstrates the power of word-of-mouth marketing. It reports that the percentage of brand-related opinions expressed to either family or friends is 72 per cent; and that 41 per cent of conversations regarding brands relate to an item noticed in either the media or marketing material. They also state that 62 per cent of discussions in relation to marketing are 'mostly positive' and that 9 per cent are 'mostly negeative'. And finally, that 92 per cent of word-of-mouth conversations happen offline.

> Basically we get confused a bit about what retail is. It is really just buying things, putting them on a floor and selling them.
>
> **Gerry Harvey**

Create notepads with coupon offers

Put out a notepad that people will use with coupon offers intermingled through the pages. Every now and then your customers will be surprised by a coupon for your business.

Mmmmmmm...pizza

A pizza parlour offered a two-for-one deal when people brought in their competitor's *Yellow Pages* adverts — this resulted in customers having only one pizza parlour left in their *Yellow Pages*!

Virgin

In 1986 British Airways ran a promotion to give away 5200 seats on 10 June. Always willing to be different, Virgin ran an ad that said, 'It has always been Virgin's policy to encourage you to fly to London for as little as possible. So on June 10 we encourage you to fly British Airways'. The British Airways promotion received lots of coverage and so did Virgin—and Virgin didn't have to give away 5200 seats.

People get caught up in wonderful, eye-catching pitches, but they don't do enough to close the deal. It's no good if you don't make the sale.
Donald Trump

The art of deception

An electrician who had only one truck was tired of the derision he attracted from his competitors, so he painted a different truck number on each side of his truck.

Listen to your staff

Make sure you encourage and support your staff's creativity. It was a janitor at a hotel who 'invented' the idea of external elevators (the type that are positioned on the outside of buildings) because he didn't want to lose pay while the hotel he worked at closed to install the elevator in the middle of the lobby.

Also, think back to the Post-it note and liquid paper stories.

Other ways to sell the 'G

Here are some other things I did to sell the 'G:

- ¤ I ran competitions in collector trade publications.

- ¤ I placed posters advertising the items on poster boards with 'tear-off' details.

- ¤ I branded all of my products with the <www. SportingLimitedEditions.com> address to generate awareness.

¤ I instigated a joint venture with *Collectormania* magazine and gave away ten certificates to create awareness, then added the back-end sales letter for the frames.

¤ I placed photocopies of the local newspaper article with tear-off slips with my contact details on local noticeboards around home to generate awareness.

> Business is not financial science, it's about trading ... buying and selling. It's about creating a product or service so good that people will pay for it.
>
> **Anita Roddick**

Protection

I received a letter a few months back from my accountant offering 'tax audit protection'. It only costs $22 and it will protect me for up to $1100 worth of costs if I am audited. Not a bad policy to take up at such a low price. I am sure a large number of my accountant's clients bought this insurance.

Guaranteed!

Offer your products or services with a warranty or a guarantee. If the standard in your industry is two years, offer three on your products. This shows customers that you believe you have the best-quality product and are prepared to back it up. Or simply offer a guarantee to refund your customers' money if they are not happy. Years ago when car maker Chrysler was in trouble, it began offering seven-year/70000 mile warranties, which was more than the competition. Chrysler advertised that if you want to see who builds them better, have a look at the warranty. This helped Chrysler sell a lot of cars.

Pet rocks

Pet rocks were a 1970s fad conceived by California advertising executive Gary Dahl. The first pet rocks were ordinary grey pebbles bought at a builder's supply store and marketed as if they were live pets. The fad only lasted about six months, ending with the Christmas season in December 1975. But in its short run, the pet rock made Dahl a millionaire. How's that for marketing—he sold rocks!

Twenty years and $40 billion. They seem like good round numbers.
Michael Dell

PSI

PSI is what makes a tyre strong and keeps it moving—the stronger the PSI the faster you will move forward. Build a strong PSI (product/service idea) for your business. It will allow you to move forward easier and faster. Pump up your PSI!

Make lemonade

Do you know how the home shopping industry began? A radio station took payment for a bad debt in electric can openers and then sold them on the air.

Chapter 19

From imagination to...

the ultimate business model

Key points

¤ You *don't* have to set up your business based on traditional business methods.

¤ Create a checklist that will give you *your* ultimate business. Keep your goals in mind.

¤ Include items on your ultimate business checklist that you may not be able to do now but wish to do in the future. Give yourself something to shoot for and aim high.

To tie everything together we're going to look at what I call the ultimate business model. This is a checklist I've created that incorporates a lot of what has been discussed in the book.

Traditional business

Let's start with a checklist that is *not* the ultimate business model. Following is a list of attributes that most traditional businesses have, which you want to *minimise* in your business if you possibly can. You are not going to be able to avoid all of these and in certain circumstances having or needing these things can be positive—I don't think Virgin would work without any staff!

¤ *Employees*: Having people work for you means costs and headaches—for example, superannuation, workers compensation, sick leave—it's a long list. You also have to interview and hire, and major disruptions can be caused if you hire the wrong person.

¤ *9 am to 9 pm six days a week*: Many people start their own business with the hope of freeing up time and having more flexibility but often the opposite happens.

¤ *All your savings plus a bank loan to start up*: Many people spend a large amount of money to get up and running. (When you owe the bank $100 000 you have the headaches; when you owe the bank $1 million it has the headaches.)

¤ *Limited territory*: Businesses are often started in a small pond because the owner hasn't conducted sufficient research to locate where the fish are biting.

¤ *Income limited by the number of stores*: Basing your business solely on retail outlets will give you a few ponds but they are not connected to a river or ocean.

¤ *Dependent on seasons or the economy*: Many businesses are seasonal or are disproportionately affected by factors beyond the control of the owners. For example, I know a mechanic who says that when times are tough, one of the first things people do is put off servicing their cars.

¤ *Inventory is the biggest expense*: This means low profit margins. For example, a bookshop or electronics shop must spend tens—or maybe hundreds—of thousands of dollars on stock before the doors are even opened.

¤ *Monthly leases plus utilities*: Hiring an office or retail outlet restricts cash flow.

¤ *Expensive advertising budget*: Many businesses think that expensive advertising is the best way to attract customers.

¤ *Trade time for dollars*: You are a slave to the clock, as you only get paid when you actually work (supply labour).

> You only get out of it what you put into it. If you are a sheep in this world, you're not going to get much out of it.
>
> **Greg Norman**

The ultimate business model

Now let's have a look at the *ultimate business model*. Remember, as I've said throughout the book, you must create your business according to *your own goals*, so do not take this list as being set in stone. Instead, if there are some items that don't suit you, use this list as a basis for creating your own ultimate business model that aligns with your own personal goals.

¤ *No employees*: Having no staff means lower costs and fewer headaches. If you outsource work instead of hiring people, you have more flexibility to manage workloads (no staff playing solitaire during quiet times) and you avoid the associated expenses.

¤ *Set your own hours*: Design your business systems so that you can work when you want to and avoid becoming a slave to traditional business hours. Remember that you don't necessarily have to be available from nine to five every day.

- *Low start-up costs*: Build a business that does not require a large outlay of capital to get started. This will ease the burden initially. You can start in your spare time if this will help.

- *No restrictions on territory*: Find a big pond to fish. Don't restrict yourself to a particular area or location. Have a website that allows you to sell overseas or team up with other businesses to expand your market.

- *Experienced mentors to advise you*: Coaching and guidance are always needed. Join organisations like those discussed in chapter 16 or find yourself a mentor through your business networks.

- *Unlimited income*: Find a large pond that has *hungry* fish. Do your homework to find your customers.

- *Recession-proof*: Create a business that will flourish no matter what the economy is doing. Find a product or service that people *always* need or offer a range of items that will enable you to sell under any economic conditions.

- *Low inventory*: Reduce cash requirements by creating a low-inventory business. Create drop-ship systems or structure payment so that you receive cash before you have to supply the product. This increases cash flow and reduces your initial capital outlay.

- *Low overheads*: This helps with cash flow. Start from home, in your spare time if necessary, and only hire staff if it's essential.

- *No advertising*: In a perfect business you would only operate at the base of the Preneur Marketing Hierarchy, with past customers and referrals. These are the easiest—and therefore cheapest—people to sell to.

- *Residual income*: Make the sale once but generate income over a set period (preferably for life!). For example, sell your services at a low price but sign people up to contracts or rent your product out instead of selling it.

¤ *Products are included in your suite*: This means you are not just trading time for money—a doctor can only work so many hours a week but if you sell a product it can be sold without you.

> I don't want to be left behind. In fact, I want to be here before the action starts.
>
> **Kerry Packer**

When creating your own checklist, make sure it is the ultimate checklist for you. Include items that you may not be able to implement now but would like to be able to include in the future. For example, if your business is service-based, you can still write a book about your area of expertise so that you have a product to sell. Don't just create a checklist of things that will be easy for you to do now. Remember, it is the *ultimate* business model, so give yourself something to aim for.

Workbook

In the appropriate place in your From Imagination to Implementation Workbook, *create your ultimate business checklist. Refer back to the goals you have already written down.*

Conclusion

Everyone who got where he is has had to begin where he was.

Robert Louis Stevenson

Welcome to the end of the book! I hope that you have enjoyed reading it as much as I enjoyed writing it.

I've been on a wonderful ride since starting my selling the 'G venture. I've met some great people, had lots of fun, tried many new ideas and made some money. I started with a small amount of capital and built the endeavour in my spare time. I created systems that leveraged my time and money and enlisted the help of other people. I kept my cash outlays as low as possible and generated most of my sales through free publicity. I used the internet and automated the business where possible. And I often went against 'traditional' business practices. These are principles that I've also applied to the latest venture I am involved with, On Hold Advertising, and they are principles that you can use in your business, too.

Always go your own way and create a business that lets you live the life you want. Don't be afraid to be different, to make yourself stand out. Otherwise, how will you get ahead of the pack? You will no doubt encounter problems along the way, and people who will tell you that you are doing it 'wrong' or that your idea won't work. I did. But as Albert Einstein said, 'Great spirits have always encountered opposition from mediocre minds'.

I'll leave you with one final lesson — be *flexible*. We've all heard of Wrigley, the company that makes chewing gum. Well, when William Wrigley created the company, it sold soap! As an incentive for stores to carry the soap, Wrigley offered free baking powder. But the baking powder proved more popular than the soap, so Wrigley stopped making soap and began selling baking powder instead. Then Wrigley began offering stores free chewing gum with the baking powder and guess what happened...

So, the first step to business success is always to get started. Taking your idea from imagination to implementation is the key. Be prepared for twists and turns along the way and be prepared to travel wherever the journey takes you. You may not end up where you imagined but it's 100 per cent certain you will end up nowhere if you don't at least give it a go.

I wish you all the best with your entrepreneurial endeavours and hope you build a Mickey Mouse business — because Disney is a billion-dollar company.

Here's your VIP invitation to one of my seminars...

As a reader of this book, I would like to give you a massive $200 discount on one of the Preneur Marketing seminars featuring myself and a hand-selected group of leading entrepreneurs. Come along for an entire day and learn more about how to take your idea from *imagination to implementation*. Even if you already have a business, this is a must-attend so you can: keep up with the latest ideas, find out what's going on in the world of entrepreneurship and stay ahead of the competition. You'll also meet other enthusiastic businesspeople and have a chance to share ideas, and it's a great opportunity to network and form a mastermind group.

Preneur Marketing Seminars are hands-on workshops that get inside your idea and business. You may even be selected as one of our case studies and have your idea 'preneured'.

Some of the topics that are covered in-depth are:

- finding out what you stand for (USP)
- generating FREE publicity
- systemising your business
- maximising the internet
- designing your business around the Preneur Hierarchy
- and many more money-making marketing ideas.

The single goal of these unique events is to have you walk away with a tool-belt full of ideas, strategies and individual plans you can implement within 24 hours.

The full retail price to get into this inner circle is $695, which is exceptional given that's a fraction of the cost you'd typically pay to gain access to the 'Preneur Team'. However, to thank you for picking up this book and reading this far, I am willing to give you a $200 discount, meaning you can obtain access to this powerful knowledge for just $495—this includes GST, workbooks and lunch.

To book, simply put in the discount code 'VIPDISC' when you book online at <www.preneurmarketing.com.au>. Seminars are only run two or three times a year and to make them as effective as possible we must limit the numbers, so I suggest you book early.

Thanks again,

Pete Williams

READING THIS BOOK HAS GIVEN YOU AN EDGE OVER OTHER BUSINESSES—MAKE SURE YOU KEEP IT!

What could *you* do with some MCG carpet?

That's right, I'm running an 'Entrepreneur Challenge' to give *you* the chance to *sell the 'G*! And *keep the profits yourself*!

The challenge will consist of eight individuals or teams. You will have access to 50 pieces of genuine MCC crested carpet to market and sell any way you like. The carpet will be yours to utilise and any profits will be yours to keep. Be as creative as you like—how you sell the carpet is up to you! You will even have direct access to me for guidance and support during the challenge.

Plus, all teams who take part in the challenge will be featured in my next book.

That's right, on top of all the profits you will have a chapter of my next book dedicated to your own venture. Your idea and implementation for the carpet will be used to help others learn that there is more than one way to market a product and that it can be done part-time.

If you would like to be a part of this great opportunity, go to <www.preneurmarketing.com.au/contest.php> for more information.

This is going to be extremely popular, so get in quick!
Places are strictly limited to eight.

Index